"Dennis Johnson joins exegetical skill, theological acumen, and pastoral care to give his readers a rich treatise on Hebrews. His analysis of the genre and purpose of Hebrews leads to a portrait of Jesus that encourages weary pilgrims of every era."

Dan Doriani, Professor of Biblical and Systematic Theology, Covenant Theological Seminary

"Drawing on more than forty years of study, Dennis Johnson skillfully summarizes the main message of Hebrews with the precision of a scholar, the knowledge of a theologian, and the concern of a pastor. This volume is both profound, reflecting the central message of Jesus's superiority, and accessible, dealing with the text at a practical level. As weary pilgrims, we all need to be reminded of our perfect priest. So read this book and be greatly encouraged."

Benjamin L. Merkle, Dr. M. O. Owens Jr. Chair of New Testament Studies and Research Professor of New Testament and Greek, Southeastern Baptist Theological Seminary

"Hebrews is a master class in how to read the Bible. It shows us how all of Scripture points to Christ, explaining what God has done in Christ to save his people. Dennis Johnson is the ideal teacher to help us mine the many riches that God has given us in this 'word of exhortation.' Drawing from half a century of deep reflection on the teaching of Hebrews and from decades of pastoral ministry in the church, Johnson is a skilled and experienced guide to this biblical book. He helps us to see from Hebrews the unity of Scripture, the majesty of Christ, and the salvation that is ours in Christ, and he does so in such a way as to lead us to adore and praise our great God. Whether you have never really studied Hebrews or have been poring over Hebrews your whole life, *Perfect Priest for Weary Pilgrims* will stir you to know better that 'great high priest who has passed through the heavens, Jesus, the Son of God.'"

Guy Prentiss Waters, James M. Baird Jr. Professor of New Testament and Academic Dean, Reformed Theological Seminary, Jackson

"Dennis Johnson does a masterful job of making the daunting book of Hebrews accessible and clear. As an expert exegete, he connects the message of Hebrews to us today through a redemptive-historical lens. The fruit of reading this book is not only greater knowledge of our perfect high priest but also greater love and affection for him. I highly recommend this life-giving resource for weary pilgrims!"

Lloyd Kim, Coordinator, Mission to the World, Presbyterian Church in America

T0356003

"Dennis Johnson's treatment of the theology of Hebrews by focusing on its central theme of the (high) priesthood of Christ makes a most welcome contribution. Written out of his careful study of many years, it serves a broad audience. Both those with a beginning interest in what Hebrews has to teach about the person and work of Christ and those who have long treasured this teaching will read this book, as I did, with great profit."

Richard B. Gaffin Jr., Professor Emeritus of Biblical and Systematic Theology, Westminster Theological Seminary

"The book of Hebrews is a difficult nut to crack. The contemporary church often struggles with making sense of a book that is so steeped in Old Testament language and imagery. Dennis Johnson is a gifted communicator—incisive and elegant—and every time I read his writing, I learn a great deal. *Perfect Priest for Weary Pilgrims* captures the complex theology of Hebrews yet never loses sight of the book's exhortation for believers."

Benjamin L. Gladd, Executive Director, Carson Center for Theological Renewal; series editor, Essential Studies in Biblical Theology

"As a New Testament scholar, a homiletics professor, and a seasoned pastor, Dennis Johnson is ideally equipped to explore the exhortatory sermon we call Hebrews. Like the unknown author of Hebrews, he delights in exploring theology for the sake of practical application in the daily life of the Christian. In so doing he unlocks the treasures of Hebrews in a most helpful manner, giving special attention to the Christological interpretation of the Old Testament. Johnson wonderfully reveals the beauty and brilliance of Hebrews and will bring about a new appreciation of a much-neglected New Testament book."

Donald A. Hagner, George Eldon Ladd Professor Emeritus of New Testament, Fuller Theological Seminary

Perfect Priest for Weary Pilgrims

New Testament Theology

Edited by Thomas R. Schreiner and Brian S. Rosner

The Beginning of the Gospel: A Theology of Mark, Peter Orr

From the Manger to the Throne: A Theology of Luke, Benjamin L. Gladd

The Mission of the Triune God: A Theology of Acts, Patrick Schreiner

Ministry in the New Realm: A Theology of 2 Corinthians, Dane C. Ortlund

Christ Crucified: A Theology of Galatians, Thomas R. Schreiner

United to Christ, Walking in the Spirit: A Theology of Ephesians, Benjamin L. Merkle

Hidden with Christ in God: A Theology of Colossians and Philemon, Kevin W. McFadden

To Walk and to Please God: A Theology of 1 and 2 Thessalonians, Andrew S. Malone

Perfect Priest for Weary Pilgrims: A Theology of Hebrews, Dennis E. Johnson

The God Who Judges and Saves: A Theology of 2 Peter and Jude, Matthew S. Harmon

The Joy of Hearing: A Theology of the Book of Revelation, Thomas R. Schreiner

Perfect Priest for Weary Pilgrims

A Theology of Hebrews

Dennis E. Johnson

WHEATON, ILLINOIS

Published by Crossway
1300 Crescent Street
Wheaton, Illinois 60187
Cover design: Kevin Lipp
First printing 2024
Printed in the United States of America
Trade paperback ISBN: 978-1-4335-7553-2
ePub ISBN: 978-1-4335-7556-3
PDF ISBN: 978-1-4335-7554-9

Library of Congress Cataloging-in-Publication Data

Names: Johnson, Dennis E. (Dennis Edward), author.
Title: Perfect priest for weary pilgrims : a theology of Hebrews / Dennis E. Johnson.
Description: Wheaton, Illinois : Crossway, 2024. | Series: New Testament theology | Includes bibliographical references and index.
Identifiers: LCCN 2023024124 (print) | LCCN 2023024125 (ebook) | ISBN 9781433575532 (trade paperback) | ISBN 9781433575549 (pdf) | ISBN 9781433575563 (epub)
Subjects: LCSH: Bible. Hebrews—Criticism, interpretation, etc. | Bible. New Testament—Relation to the Old Testament.
Classification: LCC BS2775.52 .J53 2024 (print) | LCC BS2775.52 (ebook) | DDC 227/.8706—dc23/eng/20240311
LC record available at https://lccn.loc.gov/2023024124
LC ebook record available at https://lccn.loc.gov/2023024125

Crossway is a publishing ministry of Good News Publishers.

VP		33	32	31	30	29	28	27	26	25	24
15	14	13	12	11	10	9	8	7	6	5	4	3	2	1

To Jane—
"The heart of her husband trusts in her. . . .
She does him good . . . all the days of her life."
(Prov. 31:11–12)

Contents

Series Preface

THERE ARE REMARKABLY FEW TREATMENTS of the big ideas of single books of the New Testament. Readers can find brief coverage in Bible dictionaries, in some commentaries, and in New Testament theologies, but such books are filled with other information and are not devoted to unpacking the theology of each New Testament book in its own right. Technical works concentrating on various themes of New Testament theology often have a narrow focus, treating some aspect of the teaching of, say, Matthew or Hebrews in isolation from the rest of the book's theology.

The New Testament Theology series seeks to fill this gap by providing students of Scripture with readable book-length treatments of the distinctive teaching of each New Testament book or collection of books. The volumes approach the text from the perspective of biblical theology. They pay due attention to the historical and literary dimensions of the text, but their main focus is on presenting the teaching of particular New Testament books about God and his relations to the world on their own terms, maintaining sight of the Bible's overarching narrative and Christocentric focus. Such biblical theology is of fundamental importance to biblical and expository preaching and informs exegesis, systematic theology, and Christian ethics.

The twenty volumes in the series supply comprehensive, scholarly, and accessible treatments of theological themes from an evangelical perspective. We envision them being of value to students, preachers, and interested laypeople. When preparing an expository sermon series, for example, pastors can find a healthy supply of informative commentaries, but there are few options for coming to terms with the overall teaching of each book of the New Testament. As well as being useful in sermon and Bible study preparation, the volumes will also be of value as textbooks in college and seminary exegesis classes. Our prayer is that they contribute to a deeper understanding of and commitment to the kingdom and glory of God in Christ.

The epistle to the Hebrews frustrates and fascinates us. We may feel frustrated because the precise situation faced by the first readers differs dramatically from ours. But we are also fascinated, for we can discern, even on a first reading, that the author is a rigorous and profound thinker, one who has meditated deeply on Jesus Christ and his relationship to the Old Testament Scriptures and the Levitical cult. If we give ourselves to understand the letter, we see more clearly the glory of Jesus Christ as our prophet, priest, and king. The storyline of the Scriptures opens up to us as the relationship between the old covenant and the new covenant is unfolded. At the same time, the typological relationship between events, persons, and institutions is clarified, granting us a clearer perception of the whole counsel of God. In addition, we realize afresh that our problem with guilt and defilement has been solved through Jesus Christ's once-for-all-time sacrifice. On understanding the letter's message, we are encouraged and motivated to persevere in faith until the end of our earthly sojourn. Dennis Johnson unpacks the message of Hebrews in this wonderfully lucid and pastoral exposition of the letter. We are confident that many pastors, teachers, and lay people will want to preach, study, and share the message of Hebrews after reading his most accessible and profound treatment of this letter.

Thomas R. Schreiner and Brian S. Rosner

Preface

TRUTH BE TOLD, I did not always love Hebrews. As a young Christian and even as a seminary student, I found Hebrews daunting. It expects of its readers a deep and wide grasp of the Old Testament. Its theological reasoning is demanding to follow, even though the author rebukes his readers for needing baby's milk rather than being able to digest solid meat. It warns us against drifting to a point of apostasy from which there is no return, and that prospect is terrifying. Then there is the Greek vocabulary and syntax, which are elegant but complex. Even with the insightful guidance of Richard B. Gaffin Jr., my New Testament professor at Westminster Theological Seminary (Philadelphia), I found Hebrews a challenging mystery to crack, and I know that I was not alone.

After nine years in pastoral ministry, I was called to teach New Testament at Westminster Seminary California (WSC), and one of the courses assigned to me was General Epistles and Revelation. That meant many hours of study and classroom teaching on Hebrews; fewer classroom hours in the epistles of James, Peter, John, and Jude; and—eventually—a tentative attempt to introduce the book of Revelation (but that's another story). Over the next sixteen years, I fell in love with Hebrews, especially with its Christ-centered, redemptive-historical reading of the Old Testament. I became convinced that God's Holy Spirit has given us this letter—actually, a sermon in written form, as we will see—as a handbook and case study in discovering Christ in all the Scriptures, as the risen Jesus taught his apostles to do (Luke 24).

When the focus of my work at WSC switched to pastoral theology disciplines, a mentor encouraged me to draw on my New Testament studies in my approach to homiletics. I realized that God had been preparing me to teach homiletics in the years that he saturated my mind and heart in Hebrews and in its author's exegetical insight and pastoral sensitivity. After a decade of teaching preachers-to-be, I published *Him We Proclaim: Preaching Christ from All the Scriptures*,[1] building much of my case on Hebrews as what I called "an apostolic preaching paradigm," exemplifying the blend of Christ-centered, redemptive-historical hermeneutics and heart-searching homiletics that flows from the way Jesus himself taught his disciples to read the Old Testament. Since my retirement, I have been privileged to write two fairly brief commentaries on Hebrews[2] and to teach a course, Preaching Christ from the Epistle to the Hebrews, in the Korean-language Doctor of Ministry program offered by Westminster Theological Seminary (Philadelphia). The insightful questions raised by these faithful pastors and preachers have enriched my own grasp of Hebrews. Fifty years after graduating from seminary, I am glad to say it: I love Hebrews.

When invited to write on the theology of Hebrews for Crossway's New Testament Theology series, I was grateful for the opportunity to step back from the close reading of the text's absorbing details to view in broader perspective the theological architecture and pastoral agenda that structure and unify this New Testament treasure. I am grateful to series editors Tom Schreiner—a brother and a friend since we sat together in New Testament seminars as doctoral students in the 1970s—and Brian Rosner—a brother and a friend whom I have yet to meet in person—for this edifying assignment. I am thankful for Crossway's editorial staff, and particularly for the editorial skill and theological insight of Chris Cowan, whose questions and sug-

---

1 Dennis E. Johnson, *Him We Proclaim: Preaching Christ from All the Scriptures* (Phillipsburg, NJ: P&R, 2007).

2 Dennis E. Johnson, *Hebrews*, in *Hebrews–Revelation*, vol. 12 of *ESVEC*, ed. Iain M. Duguid, James M. Hamilton Jr., and Jay Sklar (Crossway, IL: Wheaton, 2018); Dennis E. Johnson, *Hebrews*, in The Gospel Coalition Bible Commentary, accessed May 19, 2023, https://www.thegospelcoalition.org/.

gestions have improved this book in many ways. And I am always, always grateful to our generous God for my wife, Jane—my favorite proofreader, advisor, encourager, and so much more (Prov. 31:10–31). I am awestruck by God's grace over the half-century-plus that we have shared life together.

Gentle reader, whether or not you are feeling weary, at this moment, in your pilgrimage through this world's wilderness, I can assure you that Jesus is the perfect priest who secures and supplies salvation "to the uttermost" (Heb. 7:25). My prayer is that you will come to share my love of Hebrews—better yet, to share my love for the ever-living sovereign and sympathetic Savior whose blood cleanses the conscience and to whom the Holy Spirit bears witness in this "word of exhortation" (Heb. 13:22).

Abbreviations

Ant.	*Jewish Antiquities*, by Josephus
BAGD	Bauer, Walter, William F. Arndt, F. Wilbur Gingrich, and Frederick W. Danker. *A Greek-English Lexicon of the New Testament and Other Early Christian Literature*. 2nd ed. Chicago: University of Chicago Press, 1979.
BTCP	Biblical Theology for Christian Proclamation
CBR	*Currents in Biblical Research*
CNTUOT	*Commentary on the New Testament Use of the Old Testament*. Edited by G. K. Beale and D. A. Carson. Grand Rapids, MI: Baker Academic, 2007.
ESVEC	*ESV Expository Commentary*
ET	English translation
HNTC	Harper's New Testament Commentaries
ICC	International Critical Commentary
Jub.	Jubilees
L&N	Louw, Johannes P., and Eugene A. Nida, eds. *Greek-English Lexicon of the New Testament Based on Semantic Domains*. 2nd ed. New York: United Bible Societies, 1989.
LXX	Septuagint
MT	Masoretic Text (Hebrew Scriptures)
NAC	New American Commentary

NDBT	*New Dictionary of Biblical Theology.* Edited by T. Desmond Alexander, Brian S. Rosner, D. A. Carson, and Graeme Goldsworthy. Downers Grove, IL: InterVarsity Press, 2000.
NICNT	New International Commentary on the New Testament
NIDNTTE	*New International Dictionary of New Testament Theology and Exegesis.* 5 vols. 2nd ed. Edited by Moisés Silva. Grand Rapids, MI: Zondervan Academic, 2014.
NovT	*Novum Testamentum*
NovTSup	Supplements to Novum Testamentum
NTL	New Testament Library
NTS	*New Testament Studies*
SNTSMS	Society for New Testament Studies Monograph Series
TNTC	Tyndale New Testament Commentaries
TOTC	Tyndale Old Testament Commentaries
TynBul	*Tyndale Bulletin*
WBC	Word Biblical Commentary
WTJ	*Westminster Theological Journal*

Introduction

Truth-Driven Transformation in Troubled Times

My word of exhortation.
HEBREWS 13:22

A Treasury of Truth and Encouragement

Hebrews is a rich treasury of life-transforming truth and heart-sustaining encouragement. Do you long to know Jesus of Nazareth? Hebrews introduces him as the eternal Son who radiates the glory of God (Heb. 1:2–3), the royal Messiah whom God calls "God" (1:8), and the Creator of earth and heaven (1:10–12). Hebrews also shows how close this glorious divine Son has come to you, sharing your human flesh and blood (2:9–16), enduring suffering and trials like yours (2:17–18), and empathizing with your weakness to help you in crisis (4:15–16).

Do you long to see why Christians base all their hopes—and risk their lives—on this paradoxical union of divine majesty and human frailty in the person of Jesus? Hebrews reveals the perfection of Jesus as the one and only mediator between God and humanity, who secures our communion with God (Heb. 7:22; 8:6; 9:15). God created you for his friendship, but your bad choices have stained you to the core, creating a chasm of estrangement that you cannot cross. The Son came into the world to do God's will, enduring temptation without sinning and offering his body as the blameless sacrifice that cleanses your conscience and brings you home (4:15; 7:26; 9:14; 10:5–10). This same Son was raised from the dead (13:20), "crowned with glory and honor" (2:9), and enthroned at God's right hand (1:3, 13; 8:1). There he lives forever to pray for you (7:24–25).

Do you long to understand whether (or how) the confusing regulations and rituals about worship in Exodus and Leviticus have anything to teach us today? Hebrews helps us make sense of the interlocking system of architecture (9:1–5), priestly credentials and conduct (5:1–4; 7:11–16, 23–28), sacrificial rites (9:13–22), and sacred calendar (9:6–7; 10:1–3, 11) that God gave to Israel. Hebrews cuts through the complexity by showing that the core issue is the need to "perfect" worshipers—to cleanse the conscience, not just the flesh—so that they can approach God in his holiness (7:11, 19; 9:9–14; 10:1–4). The elaborate network in the ancient law functioned as "a shadow of the good things to come" (10:1), a preview of the ultimate conscience-cleansing event that would open the way to communion with God. Jesus's sacrifice on the cross was that watershed event (9:14; 10:10–14), so now through him we can draw near to God (4:14–16; 10:19–22).

Perhaps, recalling that the risen Lord Jesus explained to his apostles everything written about him "in the Law of Moses and the Prophets and the Psalms" (Luke 24:44), you long to see how those ancient Scriptures, given centuries before his birth in Bethlehem, foretold and foreshadowed his mission. Hebrews bursts with Old Testament passages and insightful interpretations that unveil their testimony to Jesus the Messiah. Moses testified beforehand (Heb. 3:5) to Christ's priesthood, which was foreshadowed in the mysterious Melchizedek (7:1–10; cf. Gen. 14:18–20), and the law's Levitical system prefigured Christ's singular sacrifice (Heb. 9:1–10:14). Later prophets foretold Christ's inauguration of a new covenant to surpass and displace the old, shattered covenant of Sinai (Heb. 8:5–13; cf. Jer. 31:31–34). Psalms declared the Son's superiority to angels (Heb. 1:5–13; cf. Pss. 2; 45; 97; 102; 104), his connection with humanity (Heb. 2:5–14; Ps. 8), his sacrificial obedience (Heb. 10:5–10; cf. Ps. 40), and his glorious exaltation to God's right hand (Heb. 1:3, 13; 8:1; 10:12; cf. Ps. 110). If you want to read the Old Testament the way Jesus taught his apostles to read it, watch carefully how Hebrews handles Scripture.

Do you long to discern whether your own little life and human history have meaning? Hebrews reveals a God who sovereignly controls the unfolding eras of time. He directed the flow of millennia toward the arrival of the "last days" (Heb. 1:2), the "end of the ages" when the Son entered human history "to put away sin" (9:26). The Lord still maneuvers events toward a triumphant consummation, "the world to come" (2:5) and "the city that is to come" (13:14), an unshakable kingdom (12:28) reserved for those who trust him (1:14; 6:12; 10:35–36). Covenant—a sovereignly imposed commitment between the Lord and his people—is the pattern that structures God's plan for history. So Jesus's inauguration of a new covenant, replacing the covenant mediated by Moses, brings the dawn of the era of perfection for which ancient believers longed (8:6–13; 9:8–10, 13–26). Your own life and the entire universe are directed by God's design toward a glorious destiny.

Do you find yourself weary with life's humdrum struggles, discouraged by opposition, dismayed by dangers, and doubting God's promises of a better future? Hebrews presents a realistic but hopeful paradigm to make sense of your daily experience: like the Israelite generation who left Egypt with Moses, your life is a trek through a hostile wilderness, en route to a homeland that transcends this sin-stained earth (3:7–4:13; 11:9–10, 13–16; 13:14). Hebrews strengthens drooping hands and weak knees with its display of Jesus, faith's pioneer and perfecter who endured the cross and despised its shame (12:2–3) to liberate his brothers and sisters and lead them to glory (2:10–15).

A Difficult, Daunting Enigma

But Hebrews does not yield its bounty cheaply or easily. The author acknowledges that one of his central themes—how Jesus fulfills the priesthood pattern of Melchizedek—is "hard to explain" (5:10–11). The difficulty lies not so much in the complexity of his topic but rather in the spiritual obtuseness of his audience, who "have become dull of hearing" and failed to mature spiritually (5:11–14). Nevertheless, as we turn to Hebrews from the straightforward stories in the Gospels or the theological and ethical discussions in Paul's letters, we may feel overwhelmed by a difficult, daunting enigma.

Consider the mysterious Melchizedek. This "king of Salem" and "priest of God Most High" appears briefly (three verses) in Genesis when his path crosses with Abraham's (Gen. 14:18–20). His name recurs elsewhere in the Old Testament only in Psalm 110:4, where a priestly "order" bearing his name is filled by God's oath to inaugurate a king to be a "priest forever." These two biblical texts pique our curiosity, and even the author's explanation of them poses puzzles that have been debated for millennia.

Taking a step back from Melchizedek to consider the epistle's argument as a whole, the author presupposes that his audience shares his deep and wide familiarity with Israel's ancient Scriptures. If we are not saturated in the Old Testament and its institutions, Hebrews will sound to us like a conversation conducted in a foreign language. To mine the treasures found in Hebrews, we need to invest the effort to immerse our minds in the religious heritage of ancient Israel, which was molded by the Old Testament.

Moreover, the author's interpretive strategies in exploring Old Testament texts sometimes surprise us. We may have understood Psalm 8 to describe the dignity and dominion of humanity as created in God's image in the beginning, but Hebrews presents the psalm as a promise of "the world to come," a future situation that is "not yet" (Heb. 2:5–8). In this psalm, Hebrews discerns a redemptive-historical agenda, in which man's present status, subordinate to the angels "for a little while," will lead to his being "crowned with glory and honor" (2:9). Similar redemptive-historical readings of Psalms 110 (Heb. 7:15–25) and 40 (Heb. 10:5–10) show us that we need Hebrews to teach us how the Old Testament testifies to Jesus the Christ.

Hebrews issues alarming warnings about the dire consequences of abandoning Jesus. To "drift away" (2:1), neglecting the great salvation

that the Lord announced, will incur worse punishment than that in-
flicted on the ancient law's vilest offenders (2:1–4; 10:28–31). To "fall
away," after encountering the gospel's light and the Holy Spirit's power,
is to place oneself beyond the possibility of repentance (6:4–8). Such
terrifying warnings underscore the urgency of the author's repeated
summons to "hold fast" our confidence and confession (3:6, 14; 4:14;
6:18; 10:23). But they also raise the troubling question of Christ's power
to sustain his people's faith and secure their eternal salvation. How do
we reconcile such apostasy texts with Jesus's assurance that no one can
snatch his sheep from his hand (John 10:28–29) and with the assurance
in Hebrews itself that Jesus "is able to save to the uttermost those who
draw near to God through him" (Heb. 7:25)?

Other difficulties posed by Hebrews could be mentioned, but one
more will suffice: Hebrews is obviously a communication from an author
to an audience whose past history and present challenges he[1] knows, but
its text does not identify either the author or the recipients. Unlike the
epistles of Paul, James, and Peter, Hebrews does not open with the name
of its author or the location of its addressees. Knowing the identity of a
document's author, especially if he has written other documents available to us (as Paul did), would give us a broader context for reading the
text before us. For Hebrews, however, we have no such wider context.[2]

Nor does Hebrews *explicitly* identify the location of the congregation
to which it was first written. The title "To the Hebrews" (*pros hebraious*)

---

1   That the author is male is shown by his connection of a masculine present participle with
    a first-person pronoun (*me . . . diēgoumenon*) to refer to his action: "time would fail *me
    to tell*" (11:32).

2   An ancient and widespread (but not unanimous) tradition has attributed Hebrews to
    Paul, yet the author's identification with those who heard the gospel not from the Lord
    himself but from his apostles (2:3–4) is inconsistent with Paul's claim that he received his
    apostolic calling and gospel "not from men nor through man, but through Jesus Christ
    and God the Father" (Gal. 1:1, cf. 1:11–12). Church fathers such as Origen and Reform-
    ers such as Luther and Calvin, therefore, challenged the tradition of Pauline authorship,
    as do most scholars today. For more on authorship, see Dennis E. Johnson, *Hebrews*, in
    Hebrews–Revelation, vol. 12 of *ESVEC*, ed. Iain M. Duguid, James M. Hamilton Jr., and
    Jay Sklar (Crossway, IL: Wheaton, 2018), 20–21. For a fuller discussion, see F. F. Bruce,
    The Epistle to the Hebrews, NICNT, rev. ed. (Grand Rapids, MI: Eerdmans, 1990), 14–20;
    William L. Lane, *Hebrews 1–8*, WBC 47A (Dallas: Word, 1991), xlvii–li.

was attached to the document early in its circulation. It reflects, I believe, an authentic tradition or valid inference from the contents,[3] but some scholars have argued for a Gentile audience.[4] Hebrews itself does not directly identify its recipients as either Jewish Christians or Gentile Christians, nor does it tell us where they lived.[5] When we read Philippians and 1–2 Corinthians, the accounts in the book of Acts about the founding of these churches give us insights into the situations of these churches (Acts 16, 18). Hebrews contains hints about the backstory of its recipients (Heb. 6:9–10; 10:32–34), but where they lived, how they came to trust Jesus, and what their relationship was to the author remain uncertain. Our ignorance complicates our efforts to listen to Hebrews as though we were sitting alongside its first audience.

A Catholic (General) Epistle or a "Word of Exhortation"?

One factor that contributes to our sense of the foreignness of Hebrews is its genre. Today it is placed toward the end of the New Testament in a group of writings typically called "Catholic Epistles"[6] or "General Epistles."[7] Unlike Paul's epistles to churches in Rome, Corinth, Colossae, or Thessalonica, several of these Catholic or General Epistles are addressed to congregations over broad regions (e.g., 1 Peter) or even to the Christian community at large (e.g., James, Jude). They tend not to address the distinctive difficulties of one specific congregation.

But is Hebrews a *general* epistle, addressed to far-flung Christian communities, as 1 Peter and James are? No, Hebrews addresses a congregation with a particular history. These believers had begun their Christian pilgrimage well, enduring rejection and loss (Heb. 10:32–34).

---

3   For a fuller discussion of the Hebrew/Jewish identity of the original recipients, see chap. 1.

4   Geerhardus Vos, *The Teaching of the Epistle to the Hebrews* (Grand Rapids, MI: Eerdmans, 1956), 11–19.

5   The greeting from "those who come from Italy" (13:24) may suggest an inference about the destination of Hebrews. This question will be discussed more fully in chap. 1.

6   The English "catholic" is derived directly from the Greek *katholikos*, meaning "universal," and derived in turn from the prepositional phrase *kath' holou*, *meaning* "throughout the whole."

7   On the other hand, Papyrus 46, an early manuscript of Paul's epistles (ca. AD 200), places Hebrews between Romans and 1 Corinthians, obviously assuming Pauline authorship.

But then some had grown "dull of hearing" (5:11), spiritually enfeebled, at risk of abandoning their confession altogether (2:1; 3:12; 6:4–10; 12:12–17). This congregation suffered the passing of a first generation of leaders, whom they must "remember" (13:7), and they needed to submit to their present leaders (13:17). The author hopes to visit them in person (13:19, 23). As we will see in chapter 1, the author's comments on his audience's past and present trials and his warnings and exhortations actually give us a clear picture of this congregation's spiritual situation.

Of course, the truths that Hebrews unfolds and the exhortations it issues address the needs of many churches down through the centuries, as do Paul's letters to the Corinthians, the Thessalonians, and the Philippians. But Hebrews is no more "general" or "catholic" than those very personal and passionate pastoral missives to churches in specific Greco-Roman cities.

We might also question whether "epistle" or "letter" is the literary genre that best fits Hebrews. As we have observed, Hebrews lacks the names of author and recipients that open Hellenistic epistles. The author himself describes his work as a "word of exhortation" (*tou logou tēs paraklēseōs*, 13:22). This is the expression used by a synagogue leader in Antioch in Pisidia, when, after the reading from the Law and the Prophets, he invited Paul and Barnabas, "Brothers, if you have any word of encouragement [*logos paraklēseōs*] for the people, say it" (Acts 13:15). Accepting his invitation, Paul stood and summarized Israel's history from the ancient Scriptures, leading to the announcement that from King David's "offspring God has brought to Israel a Savior, Jesus" (13:23). Paul's "word of exhortation" delivered to that synagogue congregation was an oral exposition of Old Testament Scriptures, with their application to the hearers. *It was a sermon.*

Other New Testament texts confirm that the reading of the Law and the Prophets was followed by its explanation with "exhortation" both in Jewish synagogues (Luke 4:16–21) and in Christian congregations. Paul instructs Timothy: "Until I come, devote yourself to the reading, the exhortation [*tē paraklēsei*], the teaching" (1 Tim. 4:13, my translation).

The Greek definite article with all three elements implies their regular role in the church's liturgy: Scriptures are read publicly, and then their truths are expounded and applied.[8]

How does hearing Hebrews *as a sermon* instead of reading it as a letter help us receive its message? In at least two ways. *First, since God is presently speaking, we must hear and heed.* The description "word of exhortation" alerts us to the way Hebrews calls us to *listen* to God's voice, his "living and active" and very sharp word (Heb. 4:12), as he speaks to us in the preaching of his word. Hebrews introduces quotations from the Old Testament in a way that differs from Paul. Paul typically introduces Old Testament quotations with the formula, "It is written [*gegraptai*]" (e.g., Rom. 1:17; 2:24; 3:4, 10; 4:17). By using "to write" (*graphō*) in the perfect tense, Paul emphasizes the fixed form and abiding authority of the Scriptures across generations. Written in the past, the Scriptures have abiding authority today. Hebrews, on the other hand, characteristically introduces Scripture with present tense/aspect verbs of speaking. This way of speaking envisions a situation in which God's word is being proclaimed to a gathered congregation—or, in the case of Hebrews, being read aloud in their hearing:

- "he *says* [*legei*]" (1:6, 7; 5:6; 8:8; 10:5[9])
- "the Holy Spirit *says* [*legei*]" (3:7)
- "as it *is said* [*legesthai*]" (3:15)
- "For it is witnessed [*martyreitai*] of him" (7:17)
- "the Holy Spirit also *bears witness* [*martyrei*] to us" (10:15)
- "the exhortation that *addresses* [*dialegetai*] you as sons" (12:5)

Old Testament citations are also introduced, less frequently, by verbs of speaking in past tenses, both aorist (e.g., *eipen*, 1:5; *diemartyrato*, 2:6) and perfect (e.g., *eirēken*, 1:13; 4:3). But the verb "to write" (*graphō*),

8   Further examples of the "word of exhortation" as a spoken sermon, expounding and applying Scripture, in early Christian and ancient Jewish assemblies are cited in Lane, *Hebrews 1–8*, lxx–lxxv; William L. Lane, *Hebrews 9–13*, WBC 47B (Dallas: Word, 1991), 568.

9   ESV has "he said," but the Greek verb *legei* is present: "he says."

characteristic of Paul, appears only once in Hebrews, within a Psalm 40 citation (Heb. 10:7) that, according to Hebrews, Christ *is saying* (*legei*, 10:5).[10] This word of exhortation is being read aloud to the assembled congregation, so our author writes just as he would speak if he were present among them: at this moment and in their midst, their God *is speaking* to his people through his Scriptures.

Because God is speaking this word of exhortation to us, we must listen carefully and respond faithfully to "what we have heard," the Lord's message of salvation, now conveyed to us by "those who heard" him (2:1–3). Psalm 95:7–11, which Hebrews discusses at length (3:7–4:13), expresses the author's affirmation to that early Christian congregation that God is presently speaking to them through a psalm given through David a millennium earlier. The citation opens, "*Today*, if you hear his voice" (3:7), and Hebrews draws a twofold conclusion from this. On the one hand, since the Israelite generation that left Egypt failed to enter God's "rest" through unbelief (3:16–19), "long afterward" God spoke through David in the psalm, appointing another "today," in which God's voice must be heard with faith (4:7). On the other hand, God's appointed "today" extends into the Hebrew Christians' present: "as long as it is called 'today'" they must "exhort one another every day" (3:13).

Second, the rich theology and biblical interpretation of Hebrews are aimed toward transforming lives. We are rightly impressed by the theological depth and exposition of Old Testament passages in Hebrews. So it is tempting to approach this document as a theological and hermeneutical essay with an intellectual agenda. The author's description, "word of exhortation," however, alerts us to the *profoundly pastoral purpose* toward which his biblical exposition and theological argument are directed. He aims not merely to persuade minds but also to stir and fortify hearts, to mold character, and to motivate people to faithful action.

The semantic range of the Greek word represented by "exhortation" (*paraklēsis*) is broad. Depending on its context, *paraklēsis* and its cognate verb *parakaleō* may refer to speech that (a) summons others to

---

10 In 13:22 the author acknowledges that distance requires him to preach his "word of exhortation" via writing (*epesteila*) instead of in person (see 13:19, 23).

action ("exhortation," Heb. 13:22; cf. Rom. 12:1), (b) instills confidence ("encouragement," Heb. 6:18; cf. Acts 16:40), (c) makes a request ("beg," 2 Cor. 8:4), or (d) consoles the grieving ("comfort," Matt. 5:4; 2 Cor. 1:4–7).[11] In Hebrews, the verb appears four times (3:13; 10:25; 13:19, 22) and the noun three times (6:18; 12:5; 13:22). Our author's use of this word group bridges senses (a) and (b). So he urges believers, in their interactions with each other, to "exhort one another," expressing encouragement that does not merely lift spirits but also *stimulates to perseverance* those who may be wavering in faith (3:13; 10:25).

The structure of Hebrews fits its description as a word of encouragement. The author moves through the themes of Christ's superiority to Old Testament agents of revelation (1:5–4:13), his superiority as covenant mediator to the Old Testament priesthood and sacrificial system (4:14–10:35), and as the trailblazer who leads his people into a better inheritance than Canaan (10:36–12:29). Each step in this preacher's argument for Jesus's superiority lays the theological foundation for a direct exhortation to his congregation:[12]

- Jesus surpasses the angels who conveyed God's law to Moses (1:4–14), *so pay attention to his word* (2:1–4).
- Jesus surpasses Moses, who received God's law (3:1–6), *so hear God's voice and believe his promises, unlike Moses's contemporaries* (3:7–4:13).
- Jesus surpasses Aaron as eternal high priest (4:14–5:10, 6:13–7:28), *so let us leave behind the foundation and move on to maturity* (5:11–6:12).
- Jesus's self-sacrifice and new covenant surpass the old covenant, its earthly sanctuary, and its repeated animal sacrifices (8:1–10:18), *so let us draw near to God, hold fast our confession, and support each other* (10:19–31).

11 See entries on "παράκλησις" in BAGD 618; L&N 25.150, 33.168, 33.310, 33.315; *NIDNTTE* 3:627–33.
12 On the structure of Hebrews, see R. T. France, "The Writer of Hebrews as a Biblical Expositor," *TynBul* 47, no. 2 (1996): 245–76; Johnson, *Hebrews*, 22–23, 28–30.

- Jesus leads us to the heavenly inheritance for which the patriarchs longed, which surpasses the earthly land of promise (10:32–11:40), *so let us endure in faith, looking to Jesus* (12:1–17).
- Jesus welcomes us to worship in the heavenly Mount Zion, which surpasses Sinai's terrors (12:18–24), *so let us heed his voice from heaven with thankful worship* (12:25–29).

The transition between a section of biblical and theological exposition, on the one hand, and the response it elicits, on the other, is marked by the conjunction, "therefore,"[13] followed by a second-person plural verb in the imperative mood (directly commanding the audience),[14] by a hortatory subjunctive verb ("let us," in which the author *includes himself* in the exhortation),[15] or by another verb expressing the hearers' obligation.[16]

The theological argument in each movement of the sermon is driving toward its respective exhortation section. So it is unhelpful to call any of these exhortations a "parenthesis" or a "digression"[17] that interrupts the theological discourse. Richard B. Gaffin Jr. rightly observes that the exhortation sections interspersed throughout Hebrews, rather than being interruptions, are the purpose toward which the author's argument is directed:

It is misleading to view Hebrews basically as an apologetic-polemic treatment of the person and work of Christ and the superiority of

---

13 The ESV's "therefore" accurately reflects the sense of six Greek words or constructions that introduce a conclusion drawn from the previous discussion, indicating the fitting response: *oun* (4:1, 6, 11, 14 [ESV: "then"], 16; 10:19, 35; 13:15 [ESV: "then"]); *dia touto* (2:1); *hothen* (3:1); *dio* (3:7; 6:1; 12:12, 28); *toigaroun* (12:1); and *toinyn* (13:13).

14 Heb. 3:1; 12:12–14.

15 Heb. 4:1, 11; 4:14–16; 6:1; 10:19–25; 12:1, 28; 13:13, 15.

16 Heb. 2:1. In prohibitions, the subjunctive mood in the second person (with the negative adverb *mē*, "not") functions as a second-person imperative: 3:7–8; 10:35.

17 Raymond Brown, *Christ Above All: The Message of Hebrews*, The Bible Speaks Today (Downers Grove, IL: InterVarsity Press, 1982), 46: "This *parenthesis* deals with the gospel of God. . . . In this *parenthesis* the writer reminds us of the Christian revelation of the gospel." And, strikingly: "We have already seen that 2:1–4 is a *parenthesis*. So, in order to understand the flow of the author's argument, we ought to read directly from 1:14 to 2:5, *omitting the parenthetical section*. Before his brief *digression* . . ." (53, emphasis added).

the new covenant to the old, to which various imperatives have been appended in a secondary fashion. On this view doctrine (e.g., the high priestly ministry of Christ) would be intelligible apart from considering the exhortation. Hebrews does provide profound and extensive teaching, . . . but it does that only "in solution" with application, only as the paranetic element is pervasive and shapes the course of the argument as a whole.[18]

Gaffin's observation that the teaching in Hebrews comes "in solution" with its application so that the hortatory purpose shapes the doctrinal discussion applies throughout this word of exhortation.

The central section of Hebrews (8:1–10:18), which develops the main theological subject ("the point," *kephalaion*, 8:1)—that is, Jesus's superior priestly qualification and conscience-perfecting sacrifice— is surrounded by two exhortations (4:14–16; 10:19–25) that function as bookends (*inclusio*) to the doctrinal discussion. The echoes of 4:14–16 that appear in 10:19–25 signal their interconnectedness:

- "Since we have" (*echontes oun*, 4:14; 10:19)
- "A great [high] priest" (*archierea megan*, 4:14; *hierea megan*, 10:21)
- "Jesus" (*Iēsoun*, 4:14; *Iēsou*, 10:19)
- "Let us hold fast [our/the] confession" (*kratōmen tēs homologias*, 4:14; *katechōmen tēn homologian*, 10:23)
- "Let us draw near" (*proserchōmetha*, 4:16; 10:22)
- "Confidence" (*parrēsias*, 4:16; *parrēsian*, 10:19)

Both exhortations also speak of the access into God's heavenly sanctuary that Jesus has achieved for his people. Because our "great high priest . . . has passed through the heavens" (4:14), we too may "draw near to the throne of grace" (4:16). Through Jesus's shed blood and

---

18   Richard B. Gaffin Jr., "A Sabbath Rest Still Awaits the People of God," in *Pressing toward the Mark: Essays Commemorating Fifty Years of the Orthodox Presbyterian Church*, ed. Charles G. Dennison and Richard C. Gamble (Philadelphia: Committee for the Historian of the Orthodox Presbyterian Church, 1986), 35.

sacrificed flesh, we may "enter the holy places" (10:19), drawing near with "hearts sprinkled clean from an evil conscience" (10:22). The similarities between these exhortations emphasize how both derive from Jesus's superior priestly office and sacrifice (the themes of 5:1–10:18). Because Jesus the Son is the great high priest whose once-for-all death completely cleanses consciences, believers may and must avail themselves of the access to God that Christ has won for them.

Yet these exhortations also differ from each other in ways that fit their respective locations in the sermon. As the "therefore" (*oun*) that opens 4:14 signals, this exhortation flows from motifs previously developed: (1) Jesus is "the Son of God," as the prologue (1:1–4) and Old Testament citations contrasting the Son to the angels (1:5–14) announced. (2) Jesus has been introduced as a "merciful and faithful high priest" acquainted with suffering and temptation (2:17–18). So the exhortation in 4:14–16 cites his sympathy, as one who has known temptation yet without sin. The exhortation in 10:19–25 marshals additional motivations (as its opening "therefore" implies) from the discussion of Jesus's priestly appointment and sacrificial ministry that has preceded it (5:1–10:18). Since our high priest has entered God's heavenly sanctuary, we too have confidence to enter (6:19–20; 7:24–25; 8:1–6; 9:11–12, 24–28). This confidence is based on his conscience-cleansing blood and body, sacrificed once for all to perfect those who come to God through him (9:13–14; 10:5–14). Because the author's *pastoral* purpose drives the exploration of Jesus's priesthood and sacrifice (5:1–10:18), this rich theology issues in the exhortation to draw near in confidence and hold fast our confession—and to do so corporately (10:24–25).

The description of Hebrews as a word of exhortation notifies us that its theology calls us to hear and heed its *call to respond* with enduring faith, approaching God's throne of grace and encouraging each other. Jesus said that willingness to do God's will is the prerequisite for understanding his teaching (John 7:17). That principle applies to the theology presented in Hebrews.

Agenda for Our Hearing This Word of Exhortation

Since the theology of Hebrews comes "in solution" with its application (as Gaffin observes), it's clear that the author wisely took into account, as faithful pastors do, the frame of mind and needs of the congregation whom he was addressing. So chapter 1 begins with the *situation of the original recipients*. Reminders of their past experience (6:9–10; 10:32–34), warnings about present dangers (2:1; 3:12; 4:1; 5:11–13; 6:4–9, 11–12; 10:35–38; 12:15–17), and exhortations (3:13; 10:24–25; 12:12–14) help us sketch the crisis of faith that those weary pilgrims experienced. They needed to step back and view their immediate trials in a wider perspective, as fitting the pattern of Israel's journey through the wilderness (3:7–4:11; 11:8–16; 13:14). We need to do the same.

More significant than the original audience's cultural context is their "last days" moment in the unfolding *history of revelation and redemption* (1:1–2). Chapter 2 examines how the flow of redemptive history structures God's unfolding revelation in Scripture, thereby reshaping the new covenant audience's perspective on old covenant institutions and reinforcing their own privilege and heightened responsibility. God structures the historical unfolding of his saving agenda through successive covenants, so this chapter explores the author's treatment of the components, continuities, and contrasts of divine-human covenants in the Bible.

The extensive appeal in Hebrews to the old covenant Scriptures to demonstrate the superiority of Christ illustrates the connection between *biblical interpretation* and theological discourse (which, in turn, issues in exhortation). Chapter 3 surveys the stimulating, sometimes surprising, and consistently Christ-centered approach that Hebrews takes in interpreting Old Testament texts. Shouldn't today's biblical scholars and pastors be learning from this hermeneutical example?

Chapters 4–6 explore the heart of the author's pastorally focused theology, namely, the *priestly ministry of Jesus*, by which he mediates the new covenant. In chapter 4, we observe how the Christology of Hebrews combines a robust confession of the immutable divinity of the Son (1:1–14; 4:14; 13:8) with its equally strong assertion that this divine Son assumed human nature, subject to weakness, temptation, and suffering, in order to rescue the children God gave him (2:5–18; 4:14–5:10). Chapter 5 discusses Jesus's priestly office "in the order of Melchizedek," noting not only its similarities to the Levitical-Aaronic priesthood but also its superiority. Chapter 6 considers how Christ's priesthood qualifies him to mediate the new covenant, promised by God through Jeremiah, in which complete forgiveness is secured. Jesus's once-for-all sacrifice of himself and entrance into heaven as the ever-living intercessor has opened access for all believers to enter the heavenly sanctuary and to worship in ways acceptable to God.

Hebrews exhorts hearers to exercise *enduring faith* in God's promises. Chapter 7 draws warning from the faithless response of Israel's wilderness generation, foreshadowing the ultimate treason of apostasy from allegiance to Jesus (Heb. 3:7–4:13; cf. 2:1–4; 6:1–8; 10:26–31). But we will also survey the role of forward-looking faith in the lives of Old Testament saints (10:35–11:40). Such faith holds fast to one's confession (4:14; 10:23) in the face of adversity and opposition. Such endurance in faith over the long run depends on consistent, proactive commitment to engage one another in congregational worship and mutual exhortation. Those who approach God through Jesus draw near to God's throne and hold fast their hope, not as independent individuals but as members of a band of pilgrims who—though weary in the wilderness—hear and heed God's summons to gather, to exhort each other, and to stimulate each other to love and good deeds (3:12–14; 10:23–25, 32–34).

1

The Wilderness Pilgrimage
of the People of God

The promise of entering his rest.

HEBREWS 4:1

Knowing Your Congregation

Good pastors know God's people. Faithful preaching demands more than orthodoxy and oratory. A biblically accurate, theologically insightful discourse delivered with eloquence is not a sermon. At least, it's not quite a sermon, since a crucial component may be missing: engagement with listeners' lives, interaction with their strengths and struggles, their joys and sorrows within, and the threats without.

Classic and contemporary discussions of preaching stress that good pastors, knowing God's people, address their sermons to their hearers' needs. In the seventeenth century, the Westminster Assembly advised the preacher, in applying the message of a biblical text, to "wisely make choice of such uses as, by his residence and conversing with his flock, he findeth most needful and seasonable; and, amongst these, such as may most draw their souls to Christ, the fountain of light, holiness, and comfort."[1] In the

---

1   *The Directory for the Publick Worship of God* (1645), in *Westminster Confession of Faith* (Glasgow: Free Presbyterian, 1976), 380–81.

nineteenth century, Patrick Fairbairn, Scottish theologian and biblical scholar, counseled pastors to visit church members' homes and to interact with them in other ways. By such personal involvement the pastor

> will thereby gain much in respect to intimacy with their state and feelings, and so become more skillful in dealing with their spiritual interests. His knowledge of them gets individualized; their distinctive tendencies and characters, . . . the special sins and temptations which they need to be warned against, the duties which require to be most urgently pressed: these things . . . will get familiarized to the mind of the pastor.[2]

In the twenty-first century, after decades of ministry in such disparate contexts as rural Virginia and New York City, Timothy Keller counsels preachers,

> When you read the text and write the sermon, think specifically of individuals you know with various spiritual conditions (non-Christian, weak/new Christian, strong Christian), with various besetting sins (pride, lust, worry, greed, prejudice, resentment, self-consciousness, depression, fear, guilt), and in various circumstances (loneliness, persecution, weariness, grief, sickness, failure, indecision, boredom). Now, *remembering specific faces*, look at the biblical truth you are applying and ask: *How would this text apply to this or that person?* Imagine yourself personally counseling the person with the text.[3]

The author of Hebrews is a good pastor who knows God's people. Because the author knows his hearers personally, having spent time with them in the past (13:19), he knows their "various spiritual conditions" and "various circumstances." He can remind them of their

---

2   Patrick Fairbairn, *Pastoral Theology: A Treatise on the Office and Duties of the Christian Pastor* (1875; repr., Audubon, NJ: Old Paths, 1992), 273–74.

3   Timothy Keller, *Preaching: Communicating Faith in An Age of Skepticism* (New York: Viking, 2015), 182 (emphasis in original).

strong beginning as disciples, and he can commend their ongoing faithfulness. But he also speaks pointedly about their immaturity, the possibility of lethal apostasy that threatens some of them, and the cost of discipleship they must be prepared to pay: social marginalization, public humiliation, imprisonment, homelessness, and perhaps even martyrdom.

Because Hebrews teaches theology *for the sake of exhortation*, to address the spiritual situation of a specific body of Christ followers, we open our exploration with what the book itself reveals about that first-century Jewish-Christian congregation and the challenges that they faced. Hebrews is tantalizingly reserved about this church's locale, but we can form a picture of the congregation's social situation and spiritual struggles, enabling us to hear this word of exhortation almost as though we were sitting in their assembly. We will also follow the author's lead by viewing their situation and ours in a context shared by God's people across various redemptive-historical epochs. In Moses's day, David's day, our author's day, and our day, the people of God are a band of pilgrims *traversing a wilderness* on the way to their heavenly homeland. This wider biblical-theological perspective on the life situation of believers helps us to hear God's voice addressing us with the truth that we need in our own time and place.

Crises in a Messianic Synagogue

The title, "To the Hebrews," attached to this document as early as Papyrus 46 in the second century, is probably correct: that first audience had been raised in Judaism and could trace their ancestry back to the Israelite patriarchs. Those to whom God spoke through prophets in times past were, biologically and covenantally, their "fathers" (1:1). These Hebrews had come to believe that Jesus was the royal Redeemer promised in the ancient Scriptures, the Messiah[4] to whom God had spoken the words of Psalm 2:

4 *Christos*, the Greek equivalent of the Hebrew *Mashiach* ("Messiah" or "anointed one"), appears twelve times in Hebrews (3:6, 14; 5:5; 6:1; 9:11, 14, 24, 28; 10:10; 11:26; 13:8, 21). In two of these (3:6; 5:5), "Christ" is closely associated with "Son," as in Ps. 2:2, 6–7.

You are my Son,
  today I have begotten you. (Heb. 1:5; 5:5)

They had started their Christian life confident that Jesus's death completely atoned for sins so that the animal sacrifices mandated in the law were no longer needed. Now, however, some seem to question the sufficiency of Christ's sacrifice and are casting longing looks back toward the comfortingly familiar and visible rituals of Israel's sanctuary.

These Jewish followers of Jesus would recognize the divine authority of the ancient Scriptures given to Israel. Therefore, our author builds his case for Jesus's superiority squarely on those Scriptures. Hebrews cites and explains God's ancient word from the Septuagint, the Greek version of the Old Testament widely used by Jews living outside the promised land in the Dispersion (*diaspora*, "scattering"; see John 7:35; James 1:1). They are acquainted with the law's directions for Israel's corporate worship: a sanctuary constructed according to the pattern shown to Moses on Sinai (Heb. 8:5; 9:1–4), priests authorized to enter the sanctuary (5:1–4; 7:16), and sacrifices offered by those priests on others' behalf (9:5–10; 10:1–4). The hearers know Old Testament history so well that, having recounted major stories (11:2–31), the author can allude to other Old Testament individuals and events by name or circumstance, expecting that such brief mention will bring whole narratives to mind (11:32–38). As Jews throughout the Roman Empire gathered each Sabbath in synagogues (*synagōgai*) to pray and to hear Scripture read and applied (Luke 4:15–16; Acts 9:20; 13:14–15; 18:4), so our author urges this congregation not to neglect its assembly (*episynagōgē*, ESV renders as "to meet together") for mutual exhortation (10:25).[5]

But this synagogue of messianic (Jesus-following) Jews is no longer accepted by the broader Jewish community. During Jesus's days on earth, Jews who expressed faith in him risked expulsion from synagogues (John 9:22; 12:42). Jesus warned that such rejection would escalate

---

5   Likewise, in his epistle to the "twelve tribes in the Dispersion" (James 1:1), James uses *synagōgē* to refer to an assembly of Jews who bear Jesus's name (James 2:1–2, 7).

after his death and resurrection (John 16:2), and it did (Acts 6:8–15; 13:44–50; 17:5–9; 18:4–7). The original audience of Hebrews experienced repudiation and harassment when they first came to trust in Jesus:

> But recall the former days when, after you were enlightened, you endured a hard struggle with sufferings, sometimes being publicly exposed to reproach and affliction, and sometimes being partners with those so treated. For you had compassion on those in prison, and you joyfully accepted the plundering of your property, since you knew that you yourselves had a better possession and an abiding one. (Heb. 10:32–34)

Persecutions such as these—public ridicule and humiliation, imprisonment, unjust seizure of property—were not unusual in the first Christian centuries, nor have they been down to the present (Matt. 5:10–12). Hebrews 13:12–13 suggests that, for these Jewish Christians, such hostility was associated with their expulsion from synagogues and banishment from the wider Jewish community.[6] Jesus himself "suffered outside the gate" of Jerusalem (13:12), not only geographically but also socially, ostracized from the Jewish community. Therefore, his followers must "go to him outside the camp," sharing his reproach (13:13). They must embrace exclusion and deprivation as Moses did when he forfeited royal privilege in Egypt and instead chose mistreatment with God's people—"the reproach of Christ" (11:26; see 11:24–26).

---

6 A plausible suggestion about the occasion of the audience's persecution builds on the inference that "those who come from Italy" (13:24) are expatriates residing elsewhere in the empire and conveying greetings to friends at home—that is, in Italy and perhaps in Rome itself. The earliest patristic citation of wording from Hebrews is by Clement of Rome in the last decade of the first century AD. If this inference is correct, the sufferings listed in 10:32–34 may have been associated with the edict of the Emperor Claudius in AD 49. According to the second-century Roman historian Suetonius (*Claudius* 25.4), the emperor banished the Jews from Rome because of social turmoil surrounding a certain "Chrestus" (perhaps a Roman confusion with the Greek *Christos*, suggesting discord within the Jewish community over claims that Jesus is the Messiah). Claudius's edict was God's means to bring a Jewish-Christian couple, Aquila and Priscilla, to Corinth (Acts 18:2). See William L. Lane, *Hebrews 1–8*, WBC 47A (Dallas: Word, 1991), lviii–lx, lxiii–lxvi.

In addition to the loss of acceptance, freedom, and property, their very lives were, or could soon be, at risk. Although their "struggle against sin"— to persevere in faith—had not reached the point of bloodshed (12:4), they had witnessed "the outcome" of previous leaders' faithful patterns of conduct (13:7).[7] The direction to "remember" those leaders suggests that their lives had ended, possibly by martyrdom. If martyrdom was looming, these believers especially needed to hear that God's Son became human to set free *those who had been enslaved by the fear of death* (2:14–15). External opposition—humiliation, rejection, imprisonment, material loss, violence—exerted intense pressure on the recipients of Hebrews.

Our author, however, sees greater danger in the spiritual threats looming *within* the congregation. He is encouraged by their service to the saints (6:10). But they lack maturity, and their initial zeal is flagging as they have become "dull of hearing" (5:11; see 5:12–6:3; 6:11–12).[8] If they fail to attend to the message of salvation that they have heard, they may "drift away," like a boat that slips its mooring and is carried off by the current (2:1–3). Some in the congregation are at risk of abandoning allegiance to Jesus altogether, flirting with apostasy that would prove irremediable (6:4–6; 10:28–31). To avert that disaster, they must encourage each other constantly:[9]

- "Take care, brothers, lest there be in any of you [*mēpote estai en tini hymōn*] an evil, unbelieving heart, leading you to *fall away* from the living God. But exhort one another every day, as long as it is called 'today,' that none of you [*hina mē . . . tis ex hymōn*] may be *hardened by the deceitfulness of sin*" (3:12–13).
- "Therefore, while the promise of entering his rest still stands, let us fear lest any of you [*mēpote . . . tis ex hymōn*] should seem to have *failed to reach* it" (4:1).

7 The past (aorist) tense of "spoke" in 13:7 distinguishes this past generation of leaders from the congregation's present leadership, who must be respected and obeyed (13:17, 24).

8 The Greek adjective *nōthroi* appears first in "dull of hearing" (5:11) and recurs in "sluggish" (6:12).

9 The Greek negative particles *mē* and *mēpote* appear repeatedly to identify the ruinous outcome that must be avoided through persevering faith.

- "Let us therefore strive to enter that rest, so that no one [*hina mē tis*] may *fall* by the same sort of disobedience" (4:11).
- "See to it that no one [*mē tis*, "lest anyone"] *fails to obtain* the grace of God; that no [*mē tis*, "lest any"] 'root of bitterness' springs up and *causes trouble*, and by it many become *defiled*" (12:15).

This last exhortation echoes Moses's warning against hidden apostasy and idolatry (Deut. 29:18–19) and argues that unbelief can prove contagious, infecting others. The spiritual exhaustion and injury suffered by some in the congregation are expressed in vivid athletic metaphors: "Lift your drooping hands and strengthen your weak knees . . . so that what is lame may not be put out of joint but rather be healed" (12:12–13).

The apostasy that tempts the hearers involves abandoning confidence in Christ's once-for-all sacrifice and all-sufficient mediation and returning to the rituals established in the law of Moses. This is why Hebrews offers such a carefully reasoned argument for the superiority of Jesus's priestly office, sacrifice, and sanctuary to the old covenant priesthood, animal sacrifices, and tabernacle. The author reasons that, by promising a new covenant to replace the (now broken) covenant inaugurated at Sinai (Heb. 8:6–12; cf. Jer. 31:31–34), God was announcing that the first covenant was "obsolete and growing old . . . ready to vanish away" (Heb. 8:13). Now, in "these last days" (1:2), Jesus has become the mediator of this new covenant, since his death redeems his people from their transgressions under the first covenant (9:15). Christ, by offering his body in submission to God's will, "does away with" (10:9) the system of animal sacrifices altogether (see 10:5–10). Therefore, for anyone who abandons trust in God's Son and his sanctifying blood, looking elsewhere for atonement, "there no longer remains a sacrifice for sin" (10:26; see 10:26–29).

We might ask why those Hebrew Christians would be attracted to return to the law's system of Aaronic priesthood, earthly sanctuary, and animal sacrifices. One factor might have been distress over being alienated from the wider Jewish community, including their own families. Tradition and familiarity would strengthen the drawing power of the religious framework in which they had been raised. Perhaps other objections were shaking their confidence. Did Jesus's genealogy undermine his priestly credentials? About the tribe of Judah, from which Jesus descended, "Moses said nothing about priests" (7:14). Lacking genealogical descent from Levi and Aaron, "if [Jesus] were on earth, he would not be a priest at all" (8:4). Our author is prepared to answer this objection (7:11–28), but the fact that he raises it suggests that it was troubling some of his hearers.

If these Jewish believers belonged to the Dispersion, living far from the promised land, they may not have witnessed the rites performed by priests in the Jerusalem temple.[10] Yet their upbringing in Judaism and the consensus of the Jewish community (which now dismissed them as "outside the camp") may have been influencing them toward seeking spiritual reassurance in the fact that priests descended from Aaron were offering sacrificial blood incessantly in God's temple on Mount Zion, where the Lord had "put his name" centuries ago (Deut. 12:5; see 1 Kings 8:27–30). The whole system of atonement—sanctuary, priests, blood—vividly impressed the senses. It could be seen, touched, smelled, even tasted (Heb. 9:10; 13:9–10).

On the other hand, Hebrews challenges any preoccupation with the physical, visible features of the old covenant system of worship. Psalm 102:25–27 contrasts the transience of the entire created order—earth and heavens—to the immutable eternity of the Creator (Heb. 1:10–12). The whole visible universe, "not only the earth but also the heavens," is destined to be "shaken" and removed by the thundering voice of God (12:26–27). The Jerusalem temple, to which the hearers may have been tempted to return, belonged to this transient created order. It was made with hands and belonged to this creation, which is destined for destruction (9:1, 8–11, 24). Our author strives to lift his hearers' eyes higher and deeper into the reality of communion with God, anchoring

10 The law required Israelite men to converge on Jerusalem from their various tribal allotments throughout the promised land for three annual feasts (Deut. 16:16). It is unlikely that most Jews living outside the land were able to make these pilgrimages on a regular basis.

their hearts' hope in "the inner place behind the curtain, where Jesus has gone as a forerunner on our behalf" (6:19–20).

Pilgrims Traversing the Wilderness

One more dimension of this congregation's life situation is important for our understanding of Hebrews. In order to understand and respond rightly to the visible trials and threatening opposition that confront them as followers of Jesus, the congregation must see their challenges as fitting the pattern drawn centuries earlier as their ancestors sojourned in the wilderness for forty years. What we could call the "wilderness pilgrimage paradigm" for Christian living in this world is developed especially in the exposition and application of Psalm 95 in Hebrews 3:1–4:13.

Psalm 95:7–11 recalls two instances of the Israelites' rebellious unbelief in the wilderness after their liberation from slavery in Egypt. First, the "rebellion" (*parapikrasmos*[11]) and the day of "testing" (*peirasmos*) in Hebrews 3:8 (Ps. 94:8 LXX) refer to their complaint at Rephidim, even before they reached Mount Sinai, when they found no water (Ex. 17:1–7). After quenching their thirst with water from a rock, the Lord memorialized their defiant doubt by renaming the location "Massah" (*peirasmos*), which means "testing," and "Meribah" (*loidorēsis*), which means "quarreling" (Ex. 17:7 LXX).

The second incident is the people's refusal to enter the promised land at Kadesh-barnea, when they believed the hopeless report of ten spies instead of the faith-filled encouragement of Caleb and Joshua (Num. 13–14). Their refusal to trust provoked God's solemn oath that the exodus generation would not enter the land God promised to the patriarchs but would die in the desert (Num. 14:26–35; Ps. 95:9–11; see Ps. 106:24–27). The psalm, and therefore Hebrews, refers to that promised land as God's "rest." Hebrews later describes that destination as "a place that [Abraham] was to receive as an inheritance [*klēronomia*] . . . the land of promise" (Heb. 11:8–9). Hebrews follows Old Testament

---

11 Although this noun does not appear in Ex. 17 LXX as the Greek counterpart to the Hebrew *meribah*, the cognate verb is found in Deut. 31:27 LXX, where Moses summarizes Israel's history of rebellion against the Lord.

precedent when it describes the promised land as the "inheritance" promised to the patriarchs (Lev. 20:24).[12] In Hebrews, inheritance language (heir, inherit, inheritance) is associated, at least implicitly, with a homeland promised to those who trust God (Heb. 1:14 with 2:5; 6:12, 17; 9:15; 11:8–9).[13] So God's "rest," "inheritance," and "promise" all refer to the homeland that awaits people of faith.

Those who traveled in the desert with Moses were temporary residents, sojourning in a region that was not their own; but they were not wandering aimlessly, despite the delay that resulted from their obstinate unbelief at Kadesh. They were moving toward the inheritance that God had promised them. Even when the patriarchs resided in the land of promise, Abraham, Isaac, and Jacob sojourned in tents "as in a foreign land," describing themselves as "strangers and exiles on the earth" (11:9, 13; see Gen. 23:4; 47:9). In fact, Hebrews contends that the patriarchs anticipated a homeland that would transcend territory in the present, destined-for-destruction earth. They viewed from afar "the city that has foundations, whose designer and builder is God" and "a better country, that is, a heavenly one" (Heb. 11:10, 16).

The discussion of Psalm 95 in Hebrews 3–4 draws together these glimpses of the wilderness paradigm, teaching that ancient Israel's wilderness ordeal is a template for Christians' present experience. The pattern applies to three generations of God's people:

1. *Moses's generation*, who experienced the exodus but doubted in the desert and, so, failed to enter the promised land, God's "rest";
2. *David's generation*, to whom Psalm 95 was originally addressed "so long afterward" (Heb. 4:7–8), who, living in the promised land, heard God's voice in their "today" and were called to enter God's rest by trust in God's promise;

---

12 God had promised Abraham, "I am the LORD who brought you out from Ur of the Chaldeans to give you this land to possess" (Gen. 15:7). The LXX translates the Hebrew *yarash*, which the ESV renders "possess," with "inherit" (*klēronomeō*). So also LXX of Gen. 28:4; Ex. 23:30; Num. 14:24, 31; Deut. 1:8.

13 Exceptions seem to be Heb. 1:2 (the Son is the "heir of all things"); 1:4 (he "inherited" a name better than the angels); 12:17 (Esau wanted to "inherit" the blessing).

3. the *Jewish-Christian recipients of Hebrews* and all new covenant believers in Jesus, who hear God's voice "today" and must "therefore
strive to enter that rest" through enduring faith (4:7, 11; cf. 3:7,
12–15; 4:1–3).

David's psalm looks back to Israel's hard-heartedness in the wilderness and concludes that a new "today," a new moment of invitation
and testing, has arrived. Through the psalm, David's contemporaries
were hearing God's voice calling them to believe his promise, unlike
their ancestors. Hebrews, now addressing the *new covenant* people of
God (3:1), argues that this "today" of testing and invitation extends
into the present, as God's voice has spoken in a Son (1:2) and as the
Holy Spirit still speaks (3:7).

The life situations of Moses's contemporaries, the original audience
of David's psalm, and the recipients of Hebrews are linked to each other
through four parallel features: (1) an experience of *liberating grace* in
the past, (2) *God's voice* speaking in the present, (3) the *trial of faith* in
the present, and (4) the prospect of entering *God's rest* in the future.

Liberating Grace

What made the expressions of unbelief both at Massah/Meribah and
at Kadesh-barnea so heinous was that those Israelites had previously
experienced the Lord's mighty deliverance from slavery. Hebrews
highlights their culpability: "For who were those who heard and yet
rebelled? Was it not all those who left Egypt led by Moses?" (3:16)
Moreover, that unbelieving generation "saw [God's] works for forty
years" (3:9; cf. Ps. 95:9–10). Those works included not only the cloud
of God's fiery glory and the parting of the Red Sea but also water from
the rock, bread from heaven, victory in battle, the terrifying splendor
of Sinai, and more. Moses's generation had indeed experienced the
Lord's liberating grace in many ways.

Hebrews gives less attention to the liberating grace experienced by
David's contemporaries, the original audience of Psalm 95. Such grace
is implied in the mention of Joshua, whom God used to bring Israel

into the promised land and give them temporary peace from enemies (Heb. 4:7–8; see Josh. 21:43–44). (We will revisit this theme below.)

The liberating grace experienced by the recipients of Hebrews is recalled throughout this sermon. They heard the message of salvation conveyed by those who heard the Lord Jesus himself as God testified through miraculous signs (2:3–4). By the word of the gospel, God had "enlightened" them (6:4; 10:32) and gathered them to enjoy companionship with Jesus the Messiah and his Spirit (1:9; 3:14; 6:4).[14] This grace that drew them together did not, however, guarantee that every member would persevere in faith and, thus, reach the destination that God had promised. To have received God's liberating grace is a vital beginning, but more is needed to traverse the desert and enter his promised rest.

God's Voice

Hebrews seizes on the opening lines of his citation of Psalm 95,

> Today, if you hear his voice,
> do not harden your hearts (Heb. 3:7–8),

to assert that Moses's generation, David's generation, and new covenant believers share the experience of being addressed by God's word of promise and command. These two lines appear three times (3:7, 15; 4:7) in Hebrews 3:7–4:11, and the word "today" (*sēmeron*) is highlighted twice more (3:13; 4:7). As we saw in the introduction, this line expresses a twofold emphasis in Hebrews: God's word comes *in the present*, and God's word comes *in speech*, which is heard and must be heeded. God—specifically, the Holy Spirit (3:7; see 10:15)—is presently speaking to his people: to the exodus generation in the wilderness through Moses, to David's contemporaries in the promised land in Psalm 95, and now to us in these last days (Heb. 1:2).

---

14   Although the ESV and other versions use varying glosses in these three verses, Greek readers/hearers would recognize their lexical and syntactic similarity: "your companions," *tous metochous sou* (1:9); "companions of Christ," *metochoi Christou* (3:14); "companions of the Holy Spirit," *metochous . . . pneumatos hagiou* (6:4).

The content of God's speaking is "good news"—specifically, "the promise of entering his rest" (4:1–2). Elsewhere, our author also speaks of the law's commands and the penalty for violating them (2:2; 10:28), but the exposition of Psalm 95 in Hebrews 3–4 focuses on God's promise of a future homeland. Since God's voice speaks promise, he expects a response of hopeful trust.

The mode of God's speaking changes as we move from his speech to Israelites in the Sinai wilderness to his address to Jesus's followers in these last days. The Israelites heard God's voice shake the earth under their feet. Now he warns us from heaven (12:25–26) since the Son has passed through the heavens to sit at God's right hand (4:14; 8:1; 9:11–12). From his heavenly throne, the Son addresses us through faithful human leaders, who have spoken God's word in the congregation (13:7).

The most significant difference in the way God's word came in the wilderness, on the one hand, and the way it comes to us, on the other, lies in the contrast between Moses, the mediator of old covenant revelation, and Jesus, the mediator of new covenant revelation. The prelude to the exposition of Psalm 95 highlights this contrast (3:1–6). To the fathers, God spoke through Moses the faithful *servant*. Now God speaks to us through his faithful *Son*. Hebrews 3:2–4 alludes to the Lord's defense of Moses in Numbers 12:6–8: "If there is a prophet among you, I the LORD make myself known to him in a vision; I speak with him in a dream. Not so with my servant Moses. He is faithful in all my house. With him I speak mouth to mouth, clearly, and not in riddles, and he beholds the form of the LORD." Moses is a uniquely privileged recipient of divine revelation. With Moses, God speaks immediately and clearly. He commends Moses as faithful to the mission that God has entrusted to him "in all my house" (the people of God). The quality of faithfulness links Moses and "Jesus, the apostle and high priest of our confession," because Jesus too "was faithful to [God] who appointed him" for his mission (Heb. 3:1–2). Having mentioned Christ's faithfulness in his priestly calling (2:17–18), Hebrews now applies to Jesus the title "apostle"[15] to focus attention on Christ's role in revelation, the motif introduced in the sermon's prologue (1:1–4).

This prologue contrasted God's ancient speech through prophets with his last-days speech in the Son (1:1–2). Now, the superiority of Christ to Moses, the old covenant's prophet par excellence, is shown in the contrast between the titles "Son" and "servant." Moreover, Jesus is the "builder" of the "house" and "all things," whereas Moses is part of the "house" constructed by the Son (3:3–4). Contrasting prepositions "in" and "over" express the difference between servant and Son: "Moses was faithful *in* all God's house as a servant," whereas "Christ is faithful *over* God's house as a son" (3:5–6). Finally, Moses's role in revelation is not only subordinate but also preparatory for a later, better era of divine revelation: Moses was faithful "to testify to the things that *were to be spoken later*" (3:5).[16] Jesus had taught that Moses "wrote of me" (John 5:46) and that "everything written about me in the Law of Moses . . . must be fulfilled" (Luke 24:44; see also 24:27). Israel's wilderness generation and the original recipients of Hebrews heard God's voice, but the Son's divine glory demands that the latter audience pay even closer attention than those who heard Sinai's thunders.

The Trial of Faith

At both Massah and Kadesh the Israelites wrongly "tested the LORD" (Ex. 17:7; cf. Num. 14:22). In fact, though, in the wilderness the Lord was putting their hearts to the test, to reveal whether they would trust his promises and obey his commands. Moses reminded the younger generation as they were about to enter their promised inheritance: "And you shall remember the whole way that the LORD your God has led you these forty years in the wilderness, that he might humble you, testing [LXX: *ekpeirazō*] you to know what was in your heart, whether

---

15   Our author's choice of *apostolos* may reflect the influence of Jesus's statements that the Father had "sent" (*apostellō*) him into the world to accomplish his redemptive mission (John 3:34; 5:36, 38; 6:57; 7:29; 8:42; 10:36; 11:42; 17:3, 8, 18, 21, 23, 25; 20:21).

16   The ESV accurately reflects the Greek *future* passive participle, *lalēthēsomenōn*.

you would keep his commandments or not" (Deut. 8:2). The dangers of the wilderness put human hearts on trial, raising the question whether they would give greater credence to the threats their eyes could see or to the voice of the Lord they heard, which promised rest to come in an unseen future. Sadly, the generation that left Egypt with Moses failed the test of their trust. They "heard and yet rebelled . . . sinned . . . were disobedient . . . were unable to enter [God's rest] because of unbelief" (Heb. 3:16–19). Unbelief and disobedience are interrelated. To doubt God's promises breeds rebellion against his commands.

Since Moses's contemporaries "who formerly received the good news failed to enter [God's rest] because of disobedience," God announced "through David so long afterward" that he had appointed another moment of opportunity and testing, another "today" (Heb. 4:6–7). Although David's contemporaries were not wanderers in a wilderness but settlers in the promised land, the psalm announces the "today" in which they must trust God's voice, lest they, like their ancestors, fall short of God's rest. And "the promise of entering [God's] rest still stands" (4:1) not only in David's era but also in the lifetimes of the Hebrew Christian recipients of this sermon (4:3, 11). Both David's contemporaries long ago and new covenant believers in the last days are sojourning in a "wilderness" that tests their hearts.[17]

God's Rest

The final piece of the wilderness paradigm is its trajectory toward a destination in which wilderness trials are left behind and God's people enjoy rest—God's rest—glorifying and enjoying him in his presence. God's oath at Kadesh banned the unbelieving generation from entering the promised land, God's "rest" (Num. 14:21–23; Ps. 95:11; Heb. 3:11, 18; 4:1–11). The next generation, under Joshua's leadership, not only conquered the land but also experienced "rest" from warfare:

---

17   Near the end of his reign, David's prayer indicates that he shared the patriarchs' perspective of themselves as strangers who hoped for a homeland better than Canaan: "We are strangers before you and sojourners, as all our fathers were. Our days on the earth are like a shadow, and there is no abiding" (1 Chron. 29:15).

Thus the LORD gave to Israel all the land that he swore to give to their fathers. And they took possession of it, and they settled there. And the LORD *gave them rest* (MT: hiphil of *nuach*; LXX: *katapauō*) on every side just as he had sworn to their fathers. Not one of all their enemies had withstood them, for the LORD had given all their enemies into their hands. (Josh. 21:43–44)

Yet the historical background of Psalm 95 and other Scriptures gives hints that God's rest transcends the land promised to the patriarchs. The first clue that God's rest is bigger than the land of Canaan is found in Genesis. When God finished creating heaven and earth, "God rested [*katepausen*] on the seventh day from all his works" (Heb. 4:4, citing Gen. 2:2). God's rest blends his completion of labor, cessation from labor, and delight in the product of his labor. Hebrews suggests that God's rest *extends across the ages* from the completion of creation, so the opportunity for humans to enter God's rest is open to every generation.[18]

The second indication that God's rest transcends the promised land is in Hebrews 4:8: "For if Joshua had given them rest, God would not have spoken of another day later on." Although Israel had momentary rest in the land under Joshua (Josh. 21:44), the implied offer of entering God's rest extended to David's contemporaries who lived in the land suggests that God had another, better "rest" in store for those who hear his voice with faith. The interim between Joshua's (military) rest and David's (military) rest (2 Sam. 7:1), the era of Israel's judges, had been *anything but restful*, even though the Israelites were dwelling in the land promised to the patriarchs. Even when David ascended the throne and "the LORD had given him rest[19] from all his surround-

---

18 In Moses's creation account, the boundaries of the six days of creation are marked by "evening and morning," but the seventh day of God's rest is not so delimited (contrast Gen. 1:5, 8, etc., to 2:1–3). Although Hebrews does not call attention to this feature, its redefinition of "God's rest" as epoch transcending in duration is consistent with it.

19 The Hebrew original, "caused to rest" (*yanach*, hiphil of *nuach*), is interpreted "caused to inherit" (*kateklēronomēsen*) in the main LXX manuscripts. Lucian of Antioch (c. 240–312) is reported to have revised the LXX to conform the Greek text more closely

ing enemies" (2 Sam. 7:1),[20] still Israel's life in the land was troubled by their spiritual adultery and the Lord's jealous discipline through foreign enemies.

The destination that Hebrews calls "rest," drawing on the language of Psalm 95, is elsewhere described as "the city that has foundations, whose designer and builder is God," which Abraham anticipated (Heb. 11:10). It is the heavenly country that the patriarchs greeted from afar (11:13–16), the coming "lasting city" for which the new covenant audience of Hebrews hopes (13:14). Every Christian generation must recognize that, in their "today," God's voice is promising that present trials, endured with faith and hope, are leading to a homecoming of indelible joy. "We who have believed" are entering[21] God's rest (4:3), but we have not yet "rested from [our] works as God did from his" at creation (4:10). Believers are presently engaged in a lifelong process of entering God's rest through enduring faith, as we undergo the trials of the wilderness, but we have not yet arrived. Because we have not yet reached that heavenly country that God promised to the patriarchs (11:14–16), the "lasting city" that is still to come (13:14), we must "strive to enter that rest" and guard each other "so that no one may fall by the same sort of disobedience" that Moses's contemporaries displayed (4:11). Richard B. Gaffin Jr. sums up the relationship between our "today" in the wilderness and "God's rest" to come:

> "My rest," as *rest*, stands in pointed contrast to the believer's present circumstances; it is the antithesis of exposure to hardship and temptation, to the *toil* which the present involves. Believers are presently *at*

---

with the Hebrew original, and his recension apparently has "caused to rest" (*katepausen*) at 2 Sam. (2 Kgdms LXX) 7:1.

20 See also God's promise that David's son Solomon would, in fact, build God's house because "he shall be a man of rest (MT: *menuchah*; LXX: *anapauseōs*). I will give him rest (MT: *hanichoti*, hiphil of *nuach*; LXX: *anapausō*) from all his surrounding enemies" (1 Chron. 22:9; cf. 23:25).

21 A translation of the Greek *eiserchometha* in 4:3 that highlights the progressive sense of the verb's present aspect ("are entering") is preferable to the ESV's simple "we . . . enter."

work (cf. 6:10; 10:24); they are not at rest, but are strenuously seeking it (*spoudazōmen*, 4:11).[22]

Conclusion

The Jewish Christians who first received this word of exhortation had strengths and weaknesses, temptations and trials, and a social environment that set them apart from later generations of Jesus's followers. Yet the author's exposition of Psalm 95 and its commentary on Israel's wilderness generation set his first hearers' distinctives into a *theologically defined* paradigm that unites them not only with Moses's and David's generations but also with future Christian generations, including our own. Those Hebrew Christians brought to their encounter with this sermon a richer grasp of Old Testament Scriptures than we have and more vivid memories of rejection and hardship for their faith than we have endured. Yet Hebrews draws together its first-century hearers and its twenty-first century readers, linking their spiritual experience and ours by its portrayal of our shared character and context as God's redeemed pilgrims, traversing a hostile wasteland toward the haven of rest that he promises.

22 Richard B. Gaffin Jr., "A Sabbath Rest Still Awaits the People of God," in *Pressing toward the Mark: Essays Commemorating Fifty Years of the Orthodox Presbyterian Church*, ed. Charles G. Dennison and Richard C. Gamble (Philadelphia: Committee for the Historian of the Orthodox Presbyterian Church, 1986), 38. See 36–49 for Gaffin's detailed interpretation of Heb. 3:7–4:13 and his critique of the view that "God's rest" refers to Christians' present experience in this life.

The Historical Trajectory of Redemption and Revelation

These last days.

HEBREWS 1:2

What Time Is It?

The author of Hebrews has one more perspective to offer on his hearers' situation. They should not only view their sufferings through the "wilderness pilgrimage paradigm" but also recognize their temporal "location" in the unfolding history of God's redemptive plan. Getting the right answer to the question, What time is it? (i.e., Where are we in God's timeline?), is essential for grasping how God's ancient speech through the prophets serves his "last days" speech in Jesus. We live almost two thousand years later, but with respect to *God's redemptive-historical timeline*, we inhabit the same era as the original audience of Hebrews. Because God's Son has entered history, they and we together live "in these last days" (Heb. 1:2).

The living God is not a static, distant potentate. He is changeless in his infinite perfection and exempt from the flux that characterizes his universe (1:2–3, 10–12; see 13:8). But this unchanging God is proactively executing, within the flow of history, a plan that leads to the display of his glory through the rescue of his people and the re-creation of all things (1:14; 2:5–13; 12:28). Paul speaks of "the mystery of his will, according to his purpose, which he set forth in Christ as a plan for *the fullness of time,* to unite all things in him, things in heaven and things on earth" (Eph. 1:9–10).

Some of the original listeners of Hebrews were tempted to look back with longing to institutions established for ancient Israel in the law of Moses: the Levitical priesthood, the earthly sanctuary, and the animal sacrifices those priests offered in that sanctuary. But they need to recognize *the new moment* in the history of redemption and revelation that dawned when Christ "appeared once for all *at the end of the ages* to put away sin by the sacrifice of himself" (Heb. 9:26). In this chapter we see Hebrews trace the trajectory of the history of redemption and revelation, marked by a succession of divine-human covenants.

"Long Ago" versus "These Last Days"

The opening sentence of Hebrews introduces the progress of special revelation: "*Long ago,* at many times and in many ways, God spoke to our fathers by the prophets, but in these last days [*ep' eschatou tōn hēmerōn toutōn*] he has spoken to us by his Son" (1:1–2). A combination of continuity and contrast marks God's speech to humanity across the transition of historical epochs. The *continuity* lies in the affirmation that the same God who addressed the fathers through prophets has now addressed the new covenant community in the Son. The ancient Scriptures and the recent gospel proclamation originate from one God who remains the same across eons (1:10–12). Since God's prophet-speech in antiquity and his Son-speech "in these last days" come from the same immutably trustworthy Creator, his ancient words and his last days words will cohere. So our author cites words written long ago as the Holy Spirit's spoken testimony in the present (10:15–16).

The *contrast* arises from the fact that God's self-disclosure is embedded in the unfolding history of his universe. The coherence of God's ancient speech with his recent speech does not preclude progressive clarification as history advances under God's direction toward the consummation he has predetermined. In Hebrews 1:1–2, the contrast between God's prior word and his present word is threefold:

1. time frames—"long ago" and "these last days";
2. audiences—the "fathers" and "us";
3. agents of revelation—"the prophets" and the "Son."

Our author invests the time frame contrast with special theological weight by characterizing the time of God's Son-speech not as "the now" (*ta nyn*, Acts 17:30) or "the present age" (*ton kairon ton enestēkota*, Heb. 9:9)[1] but rather as "these last days" or "the last of these days" (*ep' eschatou tōn hēmerōn toutōn*, Heb. 1:2). This construction is rooted in Old Testament texts that predict the arrival of a future era, in which God will intervene to set right what human rebellion has turned terribly wrong. The divinely promised "last days," said the prophets, would display God's justice in wrath that would punish and destroy wrongdoers, and those days would unveil God's mercy and might to rescue and relieve their victims.

In the Septuagint, two constructions, *eschatē tōn hēmerōn* and *eschatai hēmerai*, reflecting the Hebrew "the end of the days" (*acherit hayammim*), appear in texts that speak of the "days to come" or "last days" in which God (who always controls history) will break into history's routine flow to bless and to judge (Gen. 49:1; Num. 24:14; Deut. 4:30; 31:29; Isa. 2:2; Jer. 23:20; Ezek. 38:16; Dan. 10:14; Mic. 4:1).[2] The

---

1   This expression in Heb. 9:9, rendered "the present age" in the ESV, may refer to the era that *was* present when the ancient tabernacle/temple, with its restricted access to the Holy Place and Most Holy Place, served as God's sanctuary on earth, the focal point of Israel's worship (this is my view; see discussion on p. 44). Alternatively, the expression may mean that God designed the tabernacle to prefigure as a symbol (*parabolē*) of "the present age" that has now arrived with the coming of Christ, which is "the time of reformation" (9:10).

2   See Geerhardus Vos, *The Pauline Eschatology* (Princeton: Princeton University Press, 1930; repr. Phillipsburg: P&R, 1994), 1–7, for a discussion of the Old Testament concept of "the end of the days" as the theological backdrop of the New Testament authors' declaration that Jesus's appearance in history has inaugurated "the last days." See also L. J. Kreitzer, "Eschatology," in *Dictionary of Paul and His Letters*, ed. Gerald F. Hawthorne, Ralph P. Martin, and Daniel G. Reid (Downers Grove, IL: InterVarsity Press, 1993), 253–69; and

prophets also used "the day of the LORD" (and "that day") to refer to the same eschatological confluence of judgment (Joel 2:1–4; Amos 5:18–20; Zeph. 1:7–16) and rescue (Isa. 4:2–6; Joel 2:28–32) that would result from the Lord's future appearance in history (Joel 3:14–20; Zech. 14:1–21; Mal. 3:16–4:3).

The New Testament announces that the incarnation, ministry, suffering, resurrection, and ascension of Jesus, God's Messiah, signal the arrival of the "last days" foretold by the prophets. On the day of Pentecost, Peter explains the church's miraculous proclamation of God's achievement in Jesus by citing a "day of the Lord" promise from Joel 2:28–32. Peter replaces Joel's generic "after this" (MT: *achare ken*; LXX: *meta tauta*) in Joel 2:28 (3:1 in MT and LXX) with an eschatologically weighted expression:

This is what was uttered through the prophet Joel:

"And *in the last days* [*en tais eschatais hēmerais*] it shall be, God
      declares,
that I will pour out my Spirit on all flesh,
and your sons and your daughters shall prophesy,
   and your young men shall see visions,
   and your old men shall dream dreams." (Acts 2:16–17)

The outpouring of God's Spirit on his people signals that "the last days" have arrived. By raising Jesus from the dead and exalting him to his right hand in heaven, God has fulfilled his promise to seat David's messianic descendant on his throne as "both Lord and Christ" (Acts 2:36; see 2:30–36).

The arrival of "the last days" is described in Hebrews 9:26: "But *now*[3] he has appeared one time *at the end of the ages* [*epi synteleia tōn*

G. K. Beale, "Eschatology," in *Dictionary of the Later New Testament and Its Developments*, ed. Ralph P. Martin and Peter H. Davids (Downers Grove, IL: InterVarsity Press, 1997), 330–45.

3   The ESV translates the Greek adverb *nyni* as "as it is" in Heb. 8:6 and 9:26, but this construction obscures the *temporal* contrast expressed by the adverb, which the CSB retains.

aiōnōn], for the removal of sin by the sacrifice of himself" (CSB). This resembles Paul's statement that the sins of Israel's wilderness generation "were written down for our instruction, on whom *the end of the ages* [*ta telē tōn aiōnōn*] has come" (1 Cor. 10:11). Thus, Hebrews answers the question, What time is it? in this way: we now live in "the last days," "the end of the ages," in which the Son has entered the world to fulfill God's will, offering his body to purge sin-stained consciences (Heb. 10:5–10) and then taking his throne at God's right hand (1:3, 13; 8:1; 10:12; 12:2).

Old Covenant versus New Covenant

The boundary between God's ancient speech in prophets and his "last days" speech in the Son is marked by the inauguration of a new covenant to replace the covenant mediated by Moses at Sinai. Jeremiah prophesied this transition: "Behold, the days are coming, declares the Lord, when I will establish a new covenant" (Heb. 8:8, quoting Jer. 31:31). Jeremiah 31:31–34 is quoted in full in Hebrews 8:8–12 and again, in part, in 10:16–17. These two citations form an *inclusio*, a literary "envelope" surrounding the discussion of the contrasts between the two covenants with respect to their promised blessings (Heb. 8:6; see 9:9–14; 10:10–14), sanctuaries (9:1–5, 8–9; see 8:1–5; 9:11–12, 21–24), and sacrifices (9:6–10, 12–14, 25–26; 10:1–14). This section of the sermon (8:1–10:17) contains fourteen of the seventeen appearances of the term "covenant" (*diathēkē*) in Hebrews.[4] In the rest of the New Testament, the term "covenant" appears only sixteen times.[5] So Hebrews contains the majority of the New Testament uses of "covenant."

---

4   The other three appearances of "covenant" (*diathēkē*) in Hebrews are also related to the Jeremiah prophecy of the new covenant and Jesus's role as mediator through his sacrificial blood: (1) By God's oath in Ps. 110:4, Jesus has become "the guarantor of a better covenant" (Heb. 7:22). (2) Jesus, "the mediator of a new covenant," and his sprinkled blood are in the heavenly Jerusalem (12:24). (3) God led up from the dead our Lord Jesus "by the blood of the eternal covenant" (13:20).

5   These are concentrated in a few discussions: Jesus's institution of the Lord's Supper (Matt. 26:28; Mark 14:24; Luke 22:20; 1 Cor. 11:25), Pauline texts contrasting the old/Mosaic covenant to the new (2 Cor. 3; Gal. 3–4; see also Rom. 11:26–27), and references to Israel's privilege as recipients of God's covenants (Acts 3:25; Rom. 9:4; Eph. 2:12). Remaining appearances include Luke 1:72–73; Acts 7:8; Rev. 11:19.

Moreover, Hebrews offers the New Testament's most extensive discussion of the relationship of the old covenant to the new. Geerhardus Vos rightly called Hebrews the epistle of the *diathēkē*.[6] The historical movement from old covenant to new is the seam that runs between God's good words of promise in a bygone era and his best and last word in the Son, fulfilling his promise in these last days.

The author to the Hebrews knows, of course, that God spoke special, redemptive words to human beings before the covenant of Sinai. God warned Noah concerning a flood to come (Heb. 11:7) and commanded Abraham to leave his homeland in Mesopotamia (11:8–13). Yet those earlier divine words have come to the Israelites, to the Hebrew Christians, and to us embedded in Moses's first book, Genesis, the historical prologue to the Sinai covenant. Moreover, although God's covenants with Noah and Abraham differ in significant ways from the covenant mediated by Moses, from the standpoint of the history of revelation, they still belong to the past era that has given way to the last days in which God has spoken in his Son. The fact that the patriarchs did not receive the fullness of the blessings promised to them shows that, at their moment in history, they could only greet those blessings from afar, as they awaited the perfection that has now arrived in Christ (11:13, 39–40).

As we saw in chapter 1, Hebrews 3:1–6 compares and contrasts Moses and the Son. Moses and Christ are alike in their faithfulness to God. But they differ in roles (Moses is *servant*; Christ is *Son*) and in relationship to the house (Moses is *in* the house; Christ is *over* the house as its Creator and Master). Moses's subordination to Christ appears especially in the redemptive-historical dimension of Moses's ministry of God's word, which was oriented toward the future: "to testify *to the things that were to be spoken later* [*lalēthēsomenōn*]" (3:5). Future tense participles are rare in the New Testament,[7] and in this occurrence the

---

6   Geerhardus Vos, "Hebrews, the Epistle of the Diatheke," in *Redemptive History and Biblical Interpretation: The Shorter Writings of Geerhardus Vos*, ed. Richard B. Gaffin Jr. (Phillipsburg, NJ: P&R, 1980), 161–233.

7   Daniel B. Wallace, *Greek Grammar Beyond the Basics: An Exegetical Syntax of the New Testament* (Grand Rapids, MI: Zondervan, 1996), 636n57, lists twelve occurrences: Matt.

tense is significant. Moses's five books contain his witness to words that *would be spoken* by God *in the future*. This far-reaching description of Moses's revelatory role resonates with Jesus's own words during his earthly ministry both to disciples (Luke 24:25–27, 44–49) and to opponents (John 5:46). While New Testament authors identify many events and institutions described in Moses's books as foreshadowing and foretelling the ministry of Christ, Hebrews focuses on those related to *priestly mediation and atonement*, as we will see. The epochal shift from old covenant to new transforms the applicability of the various categories of material found in the law of Moses. Hebrews traces this historical shift in four areas: (1) priesthood, (2) sanctuary, (3) sacrifice, and (4) promise and penalty.

Priesthood

With respect to *priestly* qualification, the law establishes the principle of genealogy—ancestral descent from Levi and Aaron—as the essential credential for service in God's ancient sanctuary. This "legal requirement concerning bodily descent" (Heb. 7:16) that set apart Aaron and his sons as legitimate priests had been announced by God himself (5:4; see Ex. 28; Lev. 8; Num. 17). As long as that covenant with its criterion for priestly appointment remained in force, Jesus would be disqualified to approach God's presence on behalf of others since he was descended not from Levi but from Judah, a tribe about which "Moses said nothing about priests" (Heb. 7:14).

Hebrews, however, finds in Psalm 110 the announcement of a different priestly order, in which qualification for service is based not on ancestry but rather on "the power of an indestructible life" (Heb. 7:16) and on God's inviolable oath (7:11, 15–22). That prophetic announcement, when it reaches fulfillment (as it has in Christ), requires "a change in the priesthood" and, consequently, "necessarily a change in the law as well" (7:12). The transition between covenants (which marks the

---

27:49; Luke 22:49; John 6:64; Acts 8:27; 20:22; 22:5; 24:11, 17; 1 Cor. 15:37; Heb. 3:5; 13:17; 1 Pet. 3:13.

transition between redemptive-historical epochs) means that "a former commandment"—specifically, the stipulation mandating descent from Levi for priestly appointment—"is set aside because of its weakness and uselessness (for the law made nothing perfect)," and in its place "a better hope is introduced, through which we draw near to God" through Jesus "the guarantor of a better covenant" (7:18–19, 22).

Sanctuary

With respect to the sanctuary in which sacrifice and intercession are offered for cleansing from sin, again the temporal shift between old covenant and new transforms the context in which the Hebrew Christians (and we) read and apply ancient Scriptures such as Exodus 25–31 and 1 Kings 6–8. Hebrews 9:1 shows the close link between the Sinai covenant and the tabernacle: "Now even the first covenant[8] had regulations for worship and an earthly place of holiness." The author looks back through history, from Herod's temple (still standing as he wrote) through the temple rebuilt after the exile and the majestic temple built by Solomon to the tabernacle (or "tent," *skēnē*) constructed at the inauguration of the covenant mediated by Moses. Hebrews notes two features linked to the redemptive-historical movement from old covenant to new. First, the *earthly* tent was "a copy and shadow" of God's *heavenly* sanctuary, which was "the pattern that was shown" to Moses "on the mountain" (8:5). Second, the *physical* relationship between the tabernacle's two chambers symbolized, for Moses and his contemporaries, the *chronological* relationship between the entire earthly tabernacle established under the old covenant and the heavenly sanctuary in which Christ, as mediator of the new covenant, now intercedes for his people (9:6–10).

---

8   The ESV appropriately supplies "covenant," since the Greek noun *diathēkē*, though unexpressed, is implied. Likewise, the ESV supplies "covenant" in 8:7 and 13 though *diathēkē* is absent in Greek. Since the citation of Jer. 31:31–34 uses *diathēkē* twice to make explicit the contrast between the coming "new covenant" (*diathēkēn kainēn*) and "the covenant [*diathēkēn*] I made with their fathers" (Heb. 8:8–9), the author expects readers to infer that he refers to covenants when he contrasts "new/better" to "first/obsolete," even when he omits the noun *diathēkē*.

The earthly tabernacle erected at Sinai was not the original locus of God's holy presence. The Levitical-Aaronic priests "serve a copy and shadow of the heavenly things" (8:5), that is, the throne room of God that transcends this physical universe. In fact, Moses himself testifies that on Sinai he was shown the template or prototype for the tabernacle: "For when Moses was about to erect the tent, he was instructed by God, saying, 'See that you make everything according to the pattern [*typos*] that was shown you on the mountain'" (8:5, citing Ex. 25:40). Hebrews 9:20–24 elaborates this perspective. The tabernacle and its utensils were "copies [*hypodeigmata*] of the heavenly things" (9:23) and "antitypes [*antitypa*] of the real things" (9:24, my translation). The original sanctuary is "heaven itself," which Christ has entered, "now to appear in the presence of God on our behalf" (9:24).

The contrast between heaven, God's true palace and throne room, and the earthly sanctuary, a replica of the original and one made by merely human hands, is grounded not only in the author's interpretation of the pattern that Moses saw on Sinai but also in other Old Testament passages, such as King Solomon's prayer at the dedication of the temple:

> But will God indeed dwell on the earth? Behold, heaven and the highest heaven cannot contain you; how much less this house that I have built! . . . Listen to the plea of your servant and of your people Israel, when they pray toward this place. And listen in *heaven your dwelling place*, and when you hear, forgive. (1 Kings 8:27, 30; see Isa. 66:1)

From the perspective of the *history of redemption*, on the one hand, the earthly tabernacle of the Mosaic covenant preceded the moment "when Christ appeared as a high priest of the good things that have come" and "through the greater and more perfect tent (not made with hands, that is, not of this creation) . . . entered once for all into the holy places" (Heb. 9:11–12). On the other hand, from the perspective of *transcendent reality*, God's heavenly holiest place, the true and ultimate sanctuary that Christ entered at his ascension, is the eternal dwelling place of God, the genuine original after which Israel's tabernacle was copied.[9]

The second aspect of the author's redemptive-historical perspective on the sanctuary is his interpretation of the physical relationship between the tabernacle's two chambers: (1) the "first section" (9:6), called "the Holy Place" (9:2), which ordinary priests entered daily, passing from the courtyard through a first curtain into the tent itself and (2) "the second section called the Most Holy Place" (9:3), which the high priest entered only on the Day of Atonement (9:7). Both chambers or sections the author to the Hebrews calls "tents" (*skēnē*), although the instruction in Exodus shows that they belong to a single enclosed structure, separated from each other only by "a veil of blue and purple and scarlet yarns and fine twined linen" (Ex. 26:31).

The adjectives "first" and "second" refer to the spatial relationship between the Holy Place and the Most Holy Place, which required priests to enter the former and the high priest to pass through that first tent to enter the second, the Most Holy Place. But Hebrews says that the two tents should be viewed as a "parable" (*parabolē*; ESV, "symbolic") with redemptive-historical significance (9:9). The first tent (*tēn protēn skēnēn*) is the venue in which many priests "regularly" perform their ritual duties (9:6). It symbolizes "the present age" (9:9)—present, that is, to old covenant Israelites, when "the way into the holy places [was] not yet opened" by the sacrifice of Christ (9:8). "As long as the first section [or "tent," *skēnē*] is still standing" (9:8)[10]—as long as that earthly tabernacle *still functions* as God's dwelling place with his people—the high priest *alone* (*monos*), only "once a year" (*hapax tou eniautou*), may enter the second tent, the Most Holy Place (9:7). The high priest's solitary and rare entrance into the second tent (9:7) aptly symbolizes the coming redemptive-historical era in which the earthly sanctuary is

---

9 See Geerhardus Vos, *The Teaching of the Epistle to the Hebrews* (Grand Rapids, MI: Eerdmans, 1956), 55–60.

10 More woodenly, 9:8 reads, "while the first tent still has [*stasin*]"—that is, "existence, continuance, standing." See "στάσις," in BAGD 764.

transcended when the eternal high priest in Melchizedek's order enters the true sanctuary *once for all* to atone for his people's sins (9:11–14). Hebrews will later contrast the ancient high priest's entrance into the Most Holy Place, which though infrequent was still repeated *every year*, to its new covenant fulfillment when Christ "appeared *once for all* [*hapax*][11] at the end of the ages to put away sin" (9:26; see 9:25–28).[12] Only with the dawn of the "time of reformation," when Christ "appeared as the high priest of the good things that *have come*" and "*entered once for all* into the holy places" (9:10–12), has access been opened for *all God's people* to "enter the holy places by the blood of Jesus" (10:19) and draw near to God (10:22).

Sacrifice

The location of the audience of Hebrews in redemptive history informs their reading of the Mosaic covenant not only with respect to the priesthood and the sanctuary but also with respect to the *sacrifices* offered at the sanctuary. Christ's singular sacrifice stands in sharp contrast to the continual slaughter of animals, "the blood of bulls and goats" (10:4), mandated by the old covenant law. That "law has but a shadow of the *good things to come* instead of the true form of these realities" (10:1). The statements in 10:2–4 show that animal sacrifices are specifically in view.

Hebrews demonstrates the insufficiency of "the blood of bulls and goats to take away sins" (10:4) and, thereby, to cleanse the conscience and perfect worshipers who draw near to God (10:1–2). The author does so by appeal to Psalm 40:6–8 (cited in Heb. 10:5–10), which he introduces as words spoken to God by the Son as he "came into the world" in his incarnation (10:5). The psalm citation consists of two pairs of antithetical parallelism. Each pair first states that the animal sacrifices were neither desired by God nor pleasing to him (a, a'). Then

---

11 Hebrews also applies the intensified adverb *ephapax* ("once for all") to Jesus's self-offering (7:27; 10:10) and his entrance into the true, heavenly "holy places" (9:12).

12 For further discussion of the exegetical issues in Heb. 9:8–10, see Dennis E. Johnson, *Hebrews*, in *Hebrews–Revelation*, vol. 12 of *ESVEC*, ed. Iain M. Duguid, James M. Hamilton Jr., and Jay Sklar (Crossway, IL: Wheaton, 2018), 122–23.

the second member of each pair articulates a different means of atonement—that is, the speaker's personal obedience—that God receives as acceptable (b, b′):

   a Sacrifices and offerings you have not desired,
     b but a body have you prepared for me;
   a′ in burnt offerings and sin offerings you have taken no pleasure.
     b′ Then I said, "Behold, I have come to do your will, O God,
          as it is written of me in the scroll of the book."

Our author's commentary gathers together the material in the a and a′ lines, first grouping the four nouns referring to animal victims—"sacrifices and offerings and burnt offerings and sin offerings"—and then grouping the verbs expressing God's displeasure—"you have neither desired nor taken pleasure" (10:8).[13] Then the author cites the psalm's b′ line, "Behold, I have come to do your will" (10:9), and alludes to the psalm's b line with "the *body* of Jesus Christ" (10:10). So the psalm juxtaposes *two means of placating God's just wrath*: on the one hand, the multiple animal sacrifices that "are offered according to the law" (10:8) and, on the other, the fulfillment of God's will by the Son who comes and assumes the "body . . . prepared for" him (10:5) to offer that body in death, "as it is written . . . in the scroll of the book" (10:7).[14]

The author's reading of Psalm 40 views this contrast through a *redemptive-historical lens*. First, the comment that the sacrifices "are offered according to the law" (Heb. 10:8) ties them to the old covenant as part of its "shadow of the good things to come" (10:1). Then, to make explicit the historical transition from that shedding of animal blood to the offering of Christ's body, our author notes that God "does away with the *first* in order to establish the *second*" (10:9). Just as the Lord's predic-

---

13 The ESV, unlike NASB and NIV, inverts the Greek word order, presumably to bring the sacrificial terms closer to the explanatory comment in 10:8: "these are offered according to the law."

14 Other Old Testament passages also contrast animal sacrifices with human obedience (or repentance) that pleases God (1 Sam. 15:22–23; Pss. 50:8–15; 51:16–17; Prov. 21:3; Isa. 1:11–20; Mic. 6:6–8).

tion that he would make a new (and better) covenant (Jer. 31:31–34) signaled that the Mosaic covenant was obsolete and ready to vanish (Heb. 8:13), so also Psalm 40 signaled that the law's *sacrificial system* would be eliminated by the Son's self-offering in death once for all.

Hebrews 9:15–20 explains why the conscience-purifying death of Christ (9:14) marks the historical shift from the old covenant to new. In Jeremiah 31, the Lord indicted Israel for breaking the old covenant. That breach of trust warranted the covenant curse that the Lord threatened to impose on his traitorous people in the wilderness (Ex. 32:7–10) and that he would eventually execute in natural disasters, invasions, and exile (Deut. 28:15–68; 2 Kings 23:26–27; 2 Chron. 36:15–21). Those who had committed "transgressions . . . under the first covenant" could be redeemed from death only by the vicarious death of a faithful, innocent, and righteous covenant keeper (Heb. 9:15). The lethal consequences of breach of covenant were graphically portrayed using blood and slain animals in the ritual by which ancient divine-human covenants were inaugurated. The author first reminds them of this death-foreshadowing covenant-ratification rite (9:16–17), and then cites as an example Moses's inauguration of the old covenant through blood at Sinai (9:18–20). Unfortunately, most English versions (and most commentators) give the impression that in 9:16–17 the legal situation in view is not a sworn bond of loyalty between living parties but rather the execution of a will after its author is deceased.[15] A better

---

15 The problem may have originated with Jerome's decision to translate the Greek term *diathēkē* in the New Testament with the Latin term *testamentum* ("last will and testament"), whereas in the Old Testament he translated the Hebrew *berith* (which the LXX represented with *diathēkē*) with the Latin terms *foedus* and *pactum* ("treaty, compact, agreement, covenant")—which are faithful counterparts to *berith*, reflecting formal agreements between living parties. In the Vulgate text of Jer. 31:31–34, for example, *foedus* and *pactum* are used as Latin equivalents of the Hebrew *berith*, whereas in the citation of the Jeremiah text in Heb. 8:8–12, the Vulgate renders the Greek term *diathēkē* (in which Hebrews is following the LXX) with the Latin *testamentum*. The result is that readers of the Vulgate receive the impression that the New Testament's use of *diathēkē* envisions the administration of an estate *after a testator's death*, rather than a blood-sealed, oath-bound commitment between living parties. In addition, grammatical and lexical complexities in Heb. 9:16–17 lead many interpreters and translators to infer that, even though *diathēkē* obviously means "covenant" in 9:15 and 18, in the intervening verses the author switches the sense of *diathēkē* from

understanding of these (admittedly difficult) verses traces a consistent line of argument from (a) the necessity of Christ's death to bring redemption for transgressions of the first (old) covenant (9:14–15) to (b) the role of death symbolism in covenant inauguration generally (9:16–17) to (c) the role of blood in the ratification of the old covenant specifically (9:18–20). A translation of 9:16–18 that reflects, very woodenly, the challenging features of the Greek text would be:

> For [gar] where a covenant [diathēkē] exists, a death of the covenant maker [diathemenou] must necessarily be brought [anangkē pheresthai]. For [gar] a covenant [diathēkē)] is confirmed [bebaia] over dead things/ones [epi nekrois[16]], since [epei] it is never in force [ischyei] when the covenant maker [diathemenos] is living. Therefore [hothen] not even the first was inaugurated without blood.

The causal, explanatory conjunctions, "for," "since," and "therefore" signal the seamless logic of the argument. Christ's death accomplished redemption for Israel's violations of the old covenant (9:15). The fact that those violations demanded death was dramatized in the ritual by which covenants were "confirmed" through the violent death of sacrificial animals, which were "brought" as symbols of the violent "death of the covenant maker," if he were to transgress the covenant (9:16). Those animal carcasses are the "dead things" over which the covenant was confirmed. Conversely, no covenant exists while a covenant maker "is living"; it only takes force when someone binds himself to maintain unswerving loyalty—or to suffer accursed death.

Hebrews is referring to the covenant-inauguration rite recorded in Genesis 15:7–20 and Jeremiah 34:8–22, in which animals were slain,

---

"covenant" to "will" (last will and testament) at 9:16, and then back to "covenant" at 9:18. Even the NASB, which rightly retains "covenant" as the English equivalent of diathēkē in Heb. 9:16–17, nevertheless translates those verses as describing the administration of a last will and testament rather than the inauguration of a covenant through death symbolism that portrays the curse that would result from transgressing the covenant.

16 Nekrois is a substantive use of the adjective nekros (dead) in the dative case (as the object of the preposition epi), plural, and either masculine or neuter in grammatical gender.

their carcasses split in half, and the halves aligned opposite each other. Then those entering the covenant walked through the dead bodies to symbolize their vow to maintain loyalty or else to endure the lethal fate suffered by the animals: "And the men who *transgressed my covenant* and did not keep the terms of the covenant that they made before me, *I will make them like the calf* that they cut in two and passed between its parts. . . . *Their dead bodies*[17] shall be food for the birds of the air and the beasts of the earth" (Jer. 34:18, 20). The central role of animal deaths, symbolizing covenant curse, in the making of biblical divine-human covenants is likewise illustrated in Moses's sprinkling of sacrificial blood when the old covenant was inaugurated at Sinai (Heb. 9:18–20). The causal conjunction "therefore" (*hothen*) in 9:18 binds this event firmly to the covenant-inauguration rite described in 9:16–17. Moses declared, "This is the blood of the covenant that God commanded for you" (9:20, citing Ex. 24:8). The Israelites had vowed, "All the words that the LORD has spoken we will do" (Ex. 24:3). The sprinkled blood put their lives on the line to keep that commitment. Too soon thereafter (Ex. 32) and repeatedly throughout both their wilderness sojourn and their life in the promised land, they broke that covenant (see Heb. 8:7–9) and kindled God's holy wrath.[18]

It is the deadly consequence of the "transgressions committed under the first covenant" (9:15)—graphically portrayed in the carcasses and blood of slain animals—that required Christ's atoning death on behalf

17 Jeremiah 41:20 LXX (34:20 MT) has neuter plural *ta thnēsimaia autōn,* "their carcasses." Similarly, Gen. 15:11, 17 LXX refers to the carcasses of the slain animals, through which the Lord passed to "cut his covenant [*dietheto . . . diathēkē*]" with Abraham by enacting a self-maledictory oath, with neuter plural substantives: *ta sōmata* ("the bodies") and *ta dichotomēmata* ("the cut-in-half things/pieces"). If, in Heb. 9:17, the *nekrois* in *epi nekrois* is grammatically neuter ("upon dead things"), it would summarize the various neuter plural terms used by the LXX to refer to animal carcasses employed in the covenant inauguration rites recorded in Gen. 15 LXX and Jer. 41 LXX (34 MT).

18 For a more detailed defense of the "covenant" interpretation of Heb. 9:16–17, in continuity with its context, see O. Palmer Robertson, *The Christ of the Covenants* (Phillipsburg, NJ: P&R, 1980), 138–44; John J. Hughes, "Hebrews IX 15ff. and Galatians III 15ff.: A Study in Covenant Practice and Procedure," *NovT* 21 (1979): 27–96; William L. Lane, *Hebrews 9–13,* WBC 47B (Dallas: Word, 1991), 242–43; Johnson, *Hebrews,* 129–31.

of guilty, but repentant, covenant violators. Having dealt with their transgressions under the old covenant by his own death, Christ is now the mediator of a new covenant (9:15), which is based on "better promises" than the old (8:6). Chief among those better promises is full and forever forgiveness of sins (8:12; 10:15–18) secured by the once-for-all self-offering of Christ on the cross (9:14; 10:12–14). So Jesus's blood erases the bitter legacy in human rebellion under the old covenant, even as it launches a new covenant, bright with better promises announced in Jeremiah 31:31–34 and summed up as "the promised eternal inheritance" (Heb. 9:15).

Promise and Penalty

The transition from old covenant to new *escalates* both the *blessings promised* to covenant keepers and the *curses threatening* those who turn away from Jesus, the new covenant mediator. The author introduces his citation of the new covenant prophecy of Jeremiah 31:31–34 by stressing that the new covenant Jesus mediates is better than the old, "since it is enacted on better *promises*" (Heb. 8:6). The Jeremiah 31 prophecy announces those "better promises":

- "I will put my laws into their minds, / and write them on their hearts" (Heb. 8:10);
- "I will be their God, / and they shall be my people" (8:10);
- "They shall all know me, / from the least of them to the greatest" (8:11);
- "I will be merciful toward their iniquities, / and I will remember their sins no more" (8:12).

The first and last of these promises are repeated at the close of the discussion of the new covenant's superiority to the old (10:15–17).

Hebrews interprets these better promises in light of the author's emphasis on access to God in worship. The first promise, that God will write his laws into *human hearts*, sets the new covenant over against Sinai, where God inscribed his commandments on *stone tablets* (Ex.

24:12; 31:18; 34:1) and where Israel, soon after vowing to obey the law (Ex. 24:3), "did not continue in my covenant" (Heb. 8:9). Elsewhere in Hebrews, the author's reassuring reflection on the readers' record of faithfulness (6:9–12; 10:32–36) shows that he shares Paul's insight that this new covenant promise is fulfilled in *the Spirit's sanctifying work* in believers' hearts (2 Cor. 3:3, 18). Yet in the theology of Hebrews, the emphasis falls on the external/internal contrast between Old Testament rites that could only "sanctify for the purification of the *flesh*" and the blood of Christ that can "purify our *conscience* . . . to serve the living God" (Heb. 9:13–14).

The second promise, "I will be their God, / and they shall be my people" (8:10), appears often in Scripture to summarize the mutual commitment between the Lord and his human subjects (Ex. 6:7; Lev. 26:12; Jer. 24:7; 32:38; Ezek. 11:20; 34:30; 37:27; Zech. 8:8; 2 Cor. 6:16; Rev. 21:3). As this promise expresses the inviolable permanence of the loving and loyal commitment of the Lord and his people, it stands in contrast to the mutual estrangement introduced by Israel's breach of the old covenant: "so I showed no concern for them" (Heb. 8:9). The new covenant is secured by God's oath-bound promise to Abraham and his oath-bound appointment of Christ as the eternal high priest to intercede ceaselessly for his people (6:13–20; 7:1–28). The new bond between the Lord and his people is unbreakable.

The third promise, that all God's people, "from the least of them to the greatest," will "know the Lord" (8:11), sets the new covenant over against the old, in which physical access to the Lord's earthly sanctuary was severely limited. By restricting who may enter the first and second tents, the Holy Spirit showed that, under the old covenant, "the way into the holy places" for all God's people was "not yet opened" (9:8). With the arrival of the new covenant through the sacrifice of Christ, "we have confidence to enter the holy places by the blood of Jesus, by the new and living way that he opened for us through the curtain, that is, through his flesh" (10:19–20). Although the new covenant community still needs leaders who teach (13:7), even "the least" believer

(8:11) can now "with confidence draw near to the throne of grace" in worship and in prayer (4:16).

The fourth promise, that God would "remember their sins no more," is the source and ground of all the previous new covenant promises, as the conjunction "for" (*hoti*) indicates (8:12). The animal sacrifices of the law could not bring forgiveness or cleansing of conscience but only provided an annual reminder of sins, since bulls' and goats' blood cannot remove sin's guilt and defilement (10:1–4). Jesus's offering of himself, by contrast, is completely sufficient to purify guilty consciences, so it took place once for all and brought an end to the perpetually re-peated animal sacrifices. When, under the new covenant, God *refuses to remember* our offenses, then "there is no longer any offering for sin" (10:18). Such complete forgiveness reaches deep into the heart (promise 1), securing the bond of love and loyalty that unite the Lord and his people (promise 2) and opening access for all believers to ap-proach their God confidently (promise 3). If, under the old covenant, the blood of slain animals could purify the flesh, "how much more will the blood of Christ . . . purify our conscience from dead works to serve the living God" (9:14).

The "how much more" escalation applies not only to the new covenant's *promises* but also to the *penalty* for violating this better covenant, spurning its mediator, and despising its blessings. Twice Hebrews reminds the audience of the grave consequences of violat-ing the old covenant law received by Moses. In both texts (2:1–4; 10:26–29) the author cites those punishments as a springboard to stress the even more severe condemnation and ruin awaiting those who violate the new covenant by committing apostasy against its majestic mediator.

The first of these two texts (2:1–4) is preceded by a series of Old Testament passages demonstrating the Son's superiority to angels. Hebrews 1:5–14 contrasts the angels' role as agents of divine revelation at Sinai with the more glorious role of the agent of revelation who, in these last days, has spoken God's message of salvation—the Son and Lord whom angels worship. The infinitely greater dignity of the Son makes disregard of his word even more culpable than transgression of the commands that angels entrusted to Moses:

> For since the message declared by angels proved to be reliable, and every transgression or disobedience received a just retribution, how shall we escape if we neglect such a great salvation? It was declared at first by the Lord, and it was attested to us by those who heard, while God also bore witness by signs and wonders and various miracles and by gifts of the Holy Spirit distributed according to his will. (2:2–4)

Deuteronomy 33:2 hints at the involvement of angels in the giving of the law at Sinai ("The Lord came from Sinai . . . from the ten thousands of holy ones"), and it is clearly taught in intertestamental Jewish sources (Jub. 1:26–2:1; Josephus, *Ant.* 15.136) and in New Testament passages (Acts 7:53; Gal. 3:19). Hebrews draws on this tradition to build a clear and cogent argument:

- When God speaks through agents of revelation, the *dignity* of those messengers reflects the *authority* of the divine word that they deliver.
- The *relative status* of the agents of divine revelation, therefore, expresses the *relative weightiness* of their messages and the *relative severity* of punishment incurred by hearers who disregard those messages.
- The role of angels, God's superhuman heavenly servants, in delivering the old covenant law to Moses, therefore, demonstrated the law's reliability and the just retribution that every transgression of its commandments deserves.
- Since God has now spoken the word of salvation in the *Lord*—the *Son* whose glory surpasses the angels' (1:3–13)—to neglect this message in the last days is to bring upon oneself *inescapable punishment.*

As redemptive history has progressed from the law declared by angels to the good news of salvation announced by the Son, the dire consequences of disregarding God's word have compounded.

The second text (10:26–29) explains in detail the just punishment imposed on those who violated the Old Testament law, the grave evil of violating the new covenant through willful apostasy, and the greater severity of punishment to be suffered by those who commit such treason against the Son of God:

> For if we go on sinning deliberately after receiving the knowledge of the truth, there no longer remains a sacrifice for sins, but a fearful expectation of judgment, and a fury of fire that will consume the adversaries. Anyone who has set aside the law of Moses dies without mercy on the evidence of two or three witnesses. How much worse punishment, do you think, will be deserved by the one who has trampled underfoot the Son of God, and has profaned the blood of the covenant by which he was sanctified, and has outraged the Spirit of grace?

The just punishment imposed on violators of the law was execution for grievous forms of rebellion: idolatry, murder, adultery and other sexual misbehavior, persistent defiance toward parents, and so on. The death penalty dramatized the seriousness of rebellion against God, and it maintained Israel's purity as a holy community.

Now under the new covenant, "sinning deliberately" refers not to disobedience to God's will generally but rather to a willful renunciation of allegiance to and trust in Jesus who is, as Paul states, the "one mediator between God and men" (1 Tim. 2:5). As we have seen, for the Hebrew Christian audience, the temptation to such apostasy would take the form of returning to the sacrificial system instituted in the Mosaic law, centered in an earthly sanctuary, administered by Levitical priests, and involving the shedding of animal blood. But the old covenant, along with its priesthood, sanctuary, and animal victims, has been rendered obsolete by the new covenant that Jesus has inaugurated (Heb. 8:13; 7:11–12, 15–19; 9:9–12; 10:1–10). At *this* moment in redemptive history, therefore, "there *no longer* remains a sacrifice for sins" (10:26)—none except the atoning sacrifice that Christ completed when he offered his body "once for all" (10:10). To turn away from Jesus, "after receiving the knowledge of the truth" (10:26), is not only to abandon the only means of reconciliation with God but also to express open contempt for the living God by trampling his Son underfoot, treating as unclean the blood he shed to sanctify his people, and outraging and insulting the Spirit of grace (10:29; cf. 6:6), whose signs and wonders were God's testimony to confirm the apostles' gospel proclamation (2:4).

The lethal consequence of defiantly violating the old covenant fore-shadowed the far greater divine vengeance brought upon oneself for apostatizing from the new covenant's gracious mediator. This worse punishment includes "a fearful expectation of judgment, and a fury of fire that will consume" God's enemies (10:27). Hebrews speaks of hell's perpetual fire less frequently than Jesus himself does (e.g., Matt. 5:22, 29–30; 10:28; 25:30, 46; Mark 9:43–47), but our author shows his sober solidarity with his Master.

The old covenant's penal sanctions were just. Some moderns find them too severe; but such an assessment reflects the anthropocentric perspective that characterizes fallen humanity generally and, specifically, the post-Enlightenment mindset that has dominated Western thought since the eighteenth century. Hebrews, by contrast, reasons that the just penalties the Mosaic law mandated for high crimes against Israel's Lord were shadowy anticipations of the even more horrific divine vengeance (10:30–31) that will—in perfect justice—punish those who despise the new covenant's glorious mediator. Just as the redemptive-historical transition from old covenant to new informs our interpretation and application of the Old Testament texts about priesthood, sanctuary, sacrifices, and covenant promises, so also Hebrews insists that the law's punishments belong to the same shadow-to-reality pattern. Although those penal sanctions belonged to the obsolete covenant that has been replaced by the new and better covenant, they pointed ahead to the eternal destruction awaiting those who turn away from Christ.[19]

19 Dennis E. Johnson, "The Epistle to the Hebrews and the Mosaic Penal Sanctions," in *Theonomy: A Reformed Critique*, ed. William S. Barker and W. Robert Godfrey (Grand Rapids, MI: Zondervan, 1990), 171–92.

"Not Yet"

Despite the differences separating new covenant members from those who lived under the old covenant, we and they have one thing in common: we have not reached the destination of our pilgrimage, the "promised eternal inheritance" (9:15). As we saw in chapter 1, the experience of Israel's wilderness generation speaks aptly to new covenant believers in our trials because we are, as they were, moving through the wilderness and have not yet fully entered God's rest. Like the patriarchs, who by faith saw and greeted from afar a heavenly city and country (11:9–16), so we await the abiding city that is still future (13:14).

The city "that is to come" (*tēn mellousan*), which Christians seek expectantly (13:14), is the focal point of "the world to come" (*tēn oikoumenēn tēn mellousan*) in which God will subject other creatures—even his glorious angels—to redeemed humankind, under the reign of Jesus, the last Adam (2:5–9).[20] To explain "the world to come," Hebrews first quotes Psalm 8:5–7 LXX (8:4–6 ET), which speaks of "man" as made "for a little while" lower than angels but subsequently "crowned with glory and honor," with "everything in subjection under his feet" (Heb. 2:6–8). The parallel between his introduction in 2:5 ("it was not to angels that God subjected the world to come") and his statement in 2:16 ("it is not angels that he helps, but . . . the offspring of Abraham") shows that our author sees in the psalm a revelation of the destiny and dignity of the human race in general. But our author interprets this psalm not as a retrospective view of the past dominion of Adam and Eve in the creation account (Gen. 1:26–28), nor as an idealized perspective on our present, post-fall situation. Rather, Hebrews hears in Psalm 8 *a forecast of the future*, when the present interruption in mankind's authority, caused by sin, is remedied. "At present [*nun*], we do *not yet* see everything in subjection to him" as it shall be in the world to come (Heb. 2:8). In the present, however, we do see Jesus, who

---

20 Paul specifically calls Christ the "last Adam" and the "second man" (1 Cor. 15:45–49; see 15:21–22), and he compares and contrasts Adam and Christ in their roles as covenant heads (Rom. 5:14–21). The interpretation of Ps. 8 in Heb. 2:6–9 also presents Adamic Christology, without explicitly mentioning humankind's original father.

in his incarnation became "for a little while . . . lower than the angels" and now, as the reward of his suffering, has been "crowned with glory and honor" (2:9). So, for Hebrews, the language of Psalm 8 forecasts Jesus's two-stage redemptive mission:

1. The Son became "for a little while[21] . . . lower than the angels" (Heb. 2:9), embracing the humble status and vulnerability experienced by his human siblings, "the offspring of Abraham" (2:16).
2. The incarnate Son was "crowned with glory and honor" because of his suffering and death on others' behalf (2:9).

Though the Hebrew Christians and we live in these last days in which the Son has come to inaugurate the new covenant, we still await the consummation of the world to come. Jesus, the last Adam, has passed through suffering to glory, "sat down at the right hand of God," and is "waiting from that time until his enemies should be made a footstool for his feet" (10:12–13).[22] So also, the siblings whom Jesus has redeemed and is leading to glory are now "eagerly waiting for him" to appear a second time in history to bring their complete salvation (9:28).

Conclusion

The audience of Hebrews needed to listen to the voice of God speaking in Scripture not only in the context of their immediate circumstances but also in the context of their privileged place in the outworking of God's redemptive plan. When the Son entered the world to offer himself as the perfect sacrifice for sin, the last days dawned. An old and broken covenant gave way to a new and better covenant. Shadows

---

21 The Greek adverb *brachy* could express a small distance (2 Sam. 16:1 LXX; Acts 27:28) or a brief interval of time (Pss. 93:17 LXX [94:17 ET], "soon"; 118:87 LXX [119:87 ET], "almost"; Luke 22:58, "a little while"; Acts 5:34, "a little while"). In Heb. 2:9, the temporal significance is clear, since Hebrews views the time frame of the Son's "inferiority" to angels as brief and now succeeded by his glorification.

22 Note the similarity of imagery expressing *complete submission*: "footstool for his feet" (Heb. 10:13, citing Ps. 109:1 LXX [110:1 ET]) and "putting everything in subjection under his feet" (Heb. 2:8, citing Ps. 8:7 LXX [8:6 ET]).

were dispelled by the arrival of realities. Realizing what time it is in God's redemptive calendar casts new light on words that God spoke long ago to the fathers through the prophets. In the ancient law, Moses bears testimony about things to be spoken in the future. The sanctuary design and the sacrifices slain point forward to the better promises secured by Jesus, the mediator and guarantor of the new covenant. This redemptive-historical situation, in which first-century Hebrew Christians stand shoulder to shoulder with twenty-first-century Christians of all nationalities, is the most significant life context for grasping the message of Hebrews.

3

The Interpretation of Ancient Scripture

Today, if you hear his voice.
HEBREWS 3:7

"The Holy Spirit Bears Witness"

No theological theme in Hebrews can be discussed without interacting with the author's interpretation of the Old Testament Scriptures. His method of exhortation (13:22) is pastoral persuasion that builds its case, at every point, on a careful reading of biblical texts.[1] He traces out the implications of what specific Scriptures say—and, on occasion, what they do not say. He challenges us to approach God's word thoughtfully, not only observing *what* is said but also reflecting on *why* it is said as it is.

In this chapter, we turn our attention to the way Hebrews opens the ancient Scriptures and demonstrates their witness to the full and final revelation that God has now spoken in his Son. This hermeneutical focus flows naturally from our exploration of the author's perspective on the unfolding history of redemption and revelation. The author of Hebrews approaches the Old Testament Scriptures with several core convictions:

---

1   R. T. France, "The Writer of Hebrews as a Biblical Expositor," *TynBul* 47, no. 2 (1996): 245–76.

1. The living God who speaks in Scripture created and sustains the universe, and he sovereignly controls human history (1:2–3, 10–12; 11:3).

2. The same God who spoke through prophets in the past has spoken in these last days in his Son (1:2–3).

3. Moses, the great prophet and mediator of the old covenant, testified in advance about the redemption and revelation that the Son, the mediator of the new and better covenant, has now brought at the end of the ages (3:1–6; 9:26).

4. As history's sovereign, God interweaves the progressive *revelation* of his redemptive purposes in Scripture with their progressive *achievement* in history. The advance of God's *redemptive accomplishment* from old covenant to new involves the advance of God's *revelatory disclosure* from shadow to reality in Christ (10:1–14).

5. Since Christ's accomplishment of redemption brings God's plan into sharper focus, God's last-days revelation in the Son unpacks the full meaning of his previous speech in the prophets.

These theological foundations undergird the author's sometimes surprising (to modern biblical scholars), eschatologically oriented understanding of such Old Testament texts as Psalm 40 (Heb. 10), as we saw in chapter 2. The difference between the hermeneutics of Hebrews and that practiced by post-Enlightenment, historical-critical (and some evangelical) scholars is undeniable.[2] The question is this:

---

2 Even France, who appreciates the writer of Hebrews as a biblical expositor, lists a series of passages in which today's interpreters demur from the author's interpretations: "Of course there are occasions when his methods differ significantly from the standard of modern historico-critical or expository methods. Few of us would wish to conclude baldly that the worship of the angels in Deuteronomy 33:43 LXX was in fact directed toward the Son (Heb. 1:6), or that the 'Lord' to whom the praise of Yahweh in Psalm 102:25–27 is addressed is in fact the Son (Heb. 1:10–12). Few modern scholars believe that, whatever the textual and lexical possibilities of the words he used, the author of Psalm 8 really intended to speak about a specific individual called 'the son of man' who would be temporarily placed below the angels (Heb. 2:8–9)." France, "The Writer of Hebrews," 273–74. In chapter 2, however, I argued that the author's use of Ps. 8 presented the psalm's *original* reference to humanity's destiny (shown in Heb. 1:14 and the parallel between 2:5

Which interpretive strategy (based on which theological presupposi-
tions) is more faithful to the Bible's claim about itself and, therefore,
more fruitful for hearing its message?

We will survey four of the author's interpretive strategies in approaching the Old Testament:

1. *If A were so, Scripture would not say B.* The wording of an Old
   Testament text presupposes that the situation in its original historical context fell short of God's best for his people. Better blessings
   were to come in the future.

2. *How much more? From good to better, bad to worse.* The consequences—for good or ill—of old covenant institutions (e.g., animal
   blood for ceremonial cleansing, curses for covenant breaches)
   foreshadow far greater consequences that result from the new
   covenant's greater blessings and curses.

3. *Scripture's silences speak.* The Holy Spirit, speaking through
   human authors, so guided their thought process and word
   choice that *even the omissions* from their narratives served
   God's purposes in providing a preview of the Son's incarnation
   and intercession.

4. *A close reading of Psalm 110.* Quotations of and allusions to
   Psalm 110 permeate Hebrews. Our author has reflected so profoundly on the specific wording of Psalm 110:1 and 4 that he
   can cite virtually every word, phrase, and clause in these verses
   to support various dimensions of his argument for the supreme
   priesthood of Christ.

If A Were So, Scripture Would Not Say B

According to Hebrews, four Old Testament passages presuppose that
the Israelites' situation *fell short of God's best* for his people when those
texts were given. If the Lord's provision at that time had been sufficient,

---

and 2:16), *not personally to Jesus* as the "son of man" but to humankind generally. *Then*
our author argued that, though we do not yet see that destiny fulfilled for humankind, we
do—by contrast—see it fulfilled already in the experience of Jesus himself.

Scripture would not have spoken as it does. Those ancient Scriptures expose the incompleteness of the old covenant order and raise expectations for the future, expectations for a perfect bond of love and loyalty to come.

The insufficiency of the old covenant: Jeremiah 31. In view of the centrality of the covenant motif, our survey begins with the author's introduction to the new covenant prophecy in Jeremiah 31:31–34 (cited in Heb. 8:8–13). Having mentioned Jesus's role as "guarantor of a better covenant" (7:22), the author connects Christ's priestly ministry to the better covenant he now mediates. The promise of this new covenant, spoken through Jeremiah at the onset of Judah's exile to Babylon, implied the fatal flaw in the covenant inaugurated at Sinai:

> For *if that first covenant had been faultless,* there would have been no occasion to look for a second.
> For he *finds fault with them* when he says:

> "Behold, the days are coming, declares the Lord,
>   when I will establish a new covenant." (8:7–8)

First, our author implies that the Sinai covenant was not "faultless" (*amemptos*),[3] but then he observes that God, speaking through the prophet, "finds fault" (*memphomenos*) with the Israelites. The blame for the breach of the first covenant lay with *the people*, not with the God-given law itself. And yet, their failure to "continue in my covenant" (8:9) revealed that the Mosaic covenant was insufficient to secure the blessings of covenant communion with God. So God gave notice—even in Jeremiah's day when that covenant was still in full force—that a new covenant, "enacted on better promises" (8:6), was needed. The Lord would establish it in days to come (8:8). By Jeremiah's prophetic word, God pronounced the first covenant "obsolete . . . growing old . . . [and] ready to vanish away" (8:13).

---

3   In its other New Testament uses, *amemptos* denotes moral or legal blamelessness (Luke 1:6; Phil. 2:15; 3:6; 1 Thess. 3:13).

The insufficiency of the promised land: Psalm 95. The same hermeneutical-theological reasoning applies to the warning spoken to David's contemporaries in Psalm 95:7–11, lest they fail to enter God's rest through unbelief (Heb. 3:7–4:11). As we have seen in chapter 1, the psalm looks back to the failure of Israel's wilderness generation to respond with faith and obedience at Kadesh-barnea, leading God to swear an oath that an entire generation would not enter his promised land (Num. 14:26–35). The psalm sums up this severe penalty:

> I swore in my wrath,
>> "They shall not enter my rest." (Heb. 3:11, citing Ps. 95:11 [94:11 LXX]; cf. Heb. 3:17–18; 4:3, 5–6)

The psalm's audience, however, included David's contemporaries, living "so long afterward" (Heb. 4:7)—not only after the rebellion at Kadesh but also after the next generation's conquest of the land under Joshua, which brought "rest" from their enemies (Josh. 21:43–45; 23:1; see 2 Sam. 7:1, 11; 1 Kings 5:4; 8:56; 2 Chron. 15:15; 20:30). If entering God's rest meant nothing more than possessing the promised land, that goal had already been achieved by the end of Joshua's leadership, generations before David wrote Psalm 95. Yet the psalm urges Israelites living in God's land, "Do not harden your hearts. Otherwise, you, like your ancestors, will be excluded by God's oath from God's rest." David's psalm would not have issued this exhortation and held out this hope to Israelites enjoying God's land unless "God's rest" transcends the land. "For if Joshua had given them rest" when he completed the conquest of the land, "God would not have spoken of another day later on" (Heb. 4:8). This other day is the "today" in which David's contemporaries were hearing God's voice in the psalm (Heb. 3:15, citing Ps. 95:7). David would not have written Psalm 95 as he did if God's rest meant nothing more than the land that Joshua conquered and David subsequently ruled. God's rest looks forward to an inheritance more transcendent than Canaan, to the "better country" that Hebrews calls "heavenly" (11:16).

The insufficiency of the Levitical priesthood: Psalm 110. Hebrews finds in Psalm 110 a signal that the ministry of Aaronic priests, who were serving when the psalm was written, fell short of what sinners need in order to be cleansed of guilt and reconciled to God (Heb. 7:11–19). Jesus and the scribes agreed that this psalm of David refers to the Messiah, David's son and royal heir (Mark 12:35–37). Later in this chapter we will survey the specifics of Christ's person and mission that Hebrews discerns in this psalm. Here, we observe that this Old Testament scripture again gives notice that another institution established in the law of Moses, the Levitical-Aaronic priesthood, failed to accomplish its purpose: "Now if perfection had been attainable through the Levitical priesthood (for under it the people received the law), what further need would there have been for another priest to arise after the order of Melchizedek, rather than one named after the order of Aaron?" (Heb. 7:11). *Perfection* refers to the cleansing of worshipers' consciences from sin's defilement, opening access to approach God's presence (9:9; 10:1). The psalm's introduction of a priest "after the order of Melchizedek" (see Ps. 110:4) implies that the priesthood of Aaron was insufficient to achieve such deep purification for worshipers. Again, Hebrews argues, "If A were so, Scripture would not say B." If Levitical priests achieved perfection for worshipers, then Psalm 110 would not announce a divine oath installing David's messianic descendant, enthroned at God's right hand (Ps. 110:1), to be priest forever *in a different order* from that of Aaron.

The insufficiency of animal sacrifices: Leviticus 16. The argument of Hebrews 10:1–4, leading to the conclusion that "it is impossible for the blood of bulls and goats to take away sins" (10:4), does not cite a specific Old Testament passage. Instead, it refers to the sacrificial practice established by the law, which mandated the repeated offering of blood every year. The mention of *annual* sacrifice shows that at this point[4] the author has in view the Day of Atonement ritual, which he had set in contrast to Christ's singular self-offering

---

4   The ceaseless repetition of *daily* sacrifices by priests other than the high priest is in view in Heb. 9:6; 10:11.

and entrance into heaven (9:24–26). That practice was grounded in the law's directions for the annual observance of repentance and reconciliation:

> And it shall be a statute to you forever that in the seventh month, on the tenth day of the month, you shall afflict yourselves and shall do no work, either the native or the stranger who sojourns among you. For on this day shall atonement be made for you to cleanse you . . . from all your sins. (Lev. 16:29–30)

Year by year, first the blood of a bull was offered for the priests' sins, and then the blood of a goat was offered for the people's sins (16:6–24)— hence, Hebrews mentions the blood of bulls and goats (Heb. 10:4). Hebrews argues that *the law's requirement* that the Day of Atonement be observed year by year is *the law's acknowledgement* (Moses's testimony; see Heb. 3:5) that animal blood could not "make perfect those who draw near" because it could not "take away sins" (10:1, 4). Thus, the author asks the rhetorical question: "*Otherwise*, would [those animal sacrifices] not have ceased to be offered, since the worshipers, having once been cleansed, would no longer have any consciousness of sins? But in these sacrifices, there is a reminder[5] of sins every year" (10:2–3). Here, the "if A were so, Scripture would not say B" reasoning takes the form, "If bulls' and goats' blood could cleanse worshipers' consciences, the sacrifices would not need to be repeated annually. The law would not have directed that such sacrifices be offered year after year on the Day of Atonement." Such ceaseless repetition stands in marked contrast to the promise of the new covenant: "I will remember their sins and their lawless deeds no more" (10:17). Christ has now "offered for all time a single sacrifice for sins" by his death (10:12), securing such complete forgiveness that henceforth "there is no longer any offering for sin" (10:18).

---

5 The annual "reminder" (*anamnēsis*) of sins demanded by the law's Day of Atonement contrasts sharply with the better new covenant promise, secured by Christ's once-for-all sacrifice: "I will *remember* [*mnēsthō*] their sins *no more*" (8:12; cf. 10:17).

How Much More? From Good to Better, Bad to Worse

We have seen (chap. 2) that the redemptive-historical transition from the old covenant to the new has entailed an escalation of consequences, both in blessing and in judgment. The blessings of God's gracious provision under the law are genuine, but they are transcended by the blessings secured by Christ for his people in the new covenant, which is "enacted on better promises" (8:6). Correspondingly, the dire consequences for violating the law delivered through angels to Moses foreshadow and are overshadowed by the more disastrous destruction awaiting those who turn their backs on the greater word of salvation spoken by the Son and sealed by his blood.

The "how much more" argument blends comparison with contrast, reasoning that a principle widely recognized as operating in a less significant instance will apply, with greater certainty and consequence, in a similar but weightier situation. Drawing inferences from a "lesser" case to a "greater" case is an interpretative principle (*qal-ve-homer*, that is, "light and heavy") that was rooted in Old Testament Scriptures and well known among the rabbis in Second Temple Judaism. It was the first of the seven interpretive principles attributed to the great rabbi Hillel.[6] Louis Jacobs cites rabbinic sources (as well as later scholars) that identify *qal-ve-homer* arguments throughout the Hebrew Scriptures— in the Law (e.g., Ex. 6:12; Deut. 31:7), the Prophets (1 Sam. 14:29–30; 2 Sam. 16:11; 1 Kings 8:27 [with Isa. 66:1]; Jer. 12:5; Jonah 4:10–11), and the Writings (Est. 9:12; Job 15:15–16; Prov. 11:31; 15:11).[7] Jacobs also notes that Jesus himself used this logic when he reasoned that, since his critics cared for their livestock's needs on the Sabbath, he had all the more justification to grant deliverance to human beings, who are more valuable than sheep (Matt. 12:11–12) and who are offspring of Abraham (Luke 13:15–16). Hebrews applies this logic when reasoning that, if sons respect human fathers whose discipline springs from finite

---

6   Richard N. Longenecker, *Biblical Exegesis in the Apostolic Period*, 2nd ed. (Grand Rapids, MI: Eerdmans, 1999), 20–21.

7   Louis Jacobs, "The 'qal va-ḥomer' Argument in the Old Testament," *Bulletin of the School of Oriental and African Studies* 35, no. 2 (1972): 221–27.

wisdom, we must "much more be subject" to the "Father of spirits," whose purpose in discipline is our eternal good: "that we may share his holiness" (Heb. 12:9–10).

"How much more" Christ's blood purifies consciences. The most significant "how much more" argument in Hebrews brings together the animal sacrifices of the old covenant and the self-offering of Christ. Just as the old covenant's sanctuary was an earthly, handmade replica of God's heavenly dwelling (8:5; 9:1), so also the animal sacrifices offered there were "a shadow of the good things to come" (10:1). So our author reasons:

> For if the blood of goats and bulls, and the sprinkling of defiled persons with the ashes of a heifer, sanctify for the purification of the flesh, *how much more* will the blood of Christ, who through the eternal Spirit offered himself without blemish to God, purify our conscience from dead works to serve the living God. (9:13–14)

The cleansing effectiveness of the sacrificial blood of bulls and goats was limited to external defilement "of the flesh." Yet such sacrifices foreshadowed Christ's infinitely superior offering, which has achieved an infinitely deeper cleansing, purifying the conscience from deeds deserving death and making worshipers acceptable to approach the living God.

"How much worse" punishment for new covenant violators. The progress of redemptive history also entails escalation from lesser to greater condemnation for refusing God's grace. The ultimate penal sanction for defiant violation of the law's gravest prohibitions was physical execution, which removed the rebel's defiling presence from God's holy community: "So you shall purge the evil from your midst" (Deut. 13:5; 17:7, 12; 21:21; 22:24). The new covenant, mediated by the Son who excels Moses the servant, imparts better blessings than the old. So anyone who repudiates this covenant, its glorious mediator, and the blood that he shed to secure its blessings deserves punishment that far exceeds physical execution:

Anyone who has set aside the law of Moses dies without mercy on the evidence of two or three witnesses. *How much worse* punishment, do you think, will be deserved by the one who has trampled underfoot the Son of God, and has profaned the blood of the covenant by which he was sanctified, and has outraged the Spirit of grace? (Heb. 10:28–29)

Our author's question makes the rhetorical point so forcefully that he does not need to elaborate what that horrific fate would involve.

Scripture's Silences Speak

Twice Hebrews draws attention to information that the Old Testament Scriptures *omit*. In both instances, the omissions are related to genealogical descent as a qualification for priestly office. The law's focus on priestly genealogy is based on the principle that God alone retains the right to appoint his priests: "No one takes this honor for himself, but only when called by God, just as Aaron was" (5:4). The priestly privilege of entering God's presence on others' behalf was not a right to be seized by self-promoting aspirants but a gift of grace sovereignly bestowed by God. So the Lord destroyed Korah, Dathan, and Abiram for their defiant demand for priestly preeminence (Num. 16). Then the blossoming of Aaron's staff—alone among rods representing Israel's tribes—confirmed God's appointment of the tribe of Levi as his sanctuary servants and of Aaron and his sons as his priests (Num. 17; cf. Heb. 9:4). By God's appointment under the old covenant, genealogical descent was *essential* to priestly qualification.

How, then, can Hebrews contend that Jesus, descendant of Judah and of David, is the new covenant mediator whose priestly ministry is "more excellent" (8:6) than that of Aaron and his descendants? After all, if Jesus "were on earth, he would not be a priest at all, since there are priests who offer gifts according to the law" in the earthly sanctuary (8:4). It is Christ's well-known genealogy that explains his disqualification to serve as priest in the *earthly* sanctuary, as a crucial omission from the Mosaic regulations about priesthood shows:

For the one of whom these things [pertaining to priestly appoint-
ment] are spoken [that is, Jesus] belonged to another tribe, from
which no one has ever served at the altar. For it is evident that our
Lord was descended from Judah, and in connection with that tribe
Moses said nothing about priests. (7:13–14)

Other New Testament texts affirm that Jesus's descent from the tribe
of Judah and the house of David is vitally important for his qualification as the messianic King (e.g., Matt. 1:1–17; 22:41–45; Luke 1:32;
3:31; Rom. 1:1–4; 2 Tim. 2:8; see 2 Sam. 7:12–16). Yet the ancestry
that establishes Jesus's legitimacy as King simultaneously *disqualifies*
him for the priesthood under the law of Moses, which never mentions God's authorization of Judah's descendants to approach him in
the sanctuary—a silence that signaled an implicit ban (see 2 Chron.
26:16–21).

The other passage in which Hebrews highlights Old Testament
omissions explains why Jesus has indeed been appointed priest by
God, despite his descent from Judah, not Levi. Psalm 110:4 introduces a different method (other than genealogical descent) by which
God appoints and authorizes a priest: an inviolable *oath*, secured
by God's own eternal life. In the only other Old Testament mention
of Melchizedek (Gen. 14:18–20)—and specifically in what that text
omits—Hebrews finds the clue that priestly authority need not de-
pend on ancestry (Heb. 7:1–10). Summarizing Moses's restraint in
narrating Abraham's encounter with "Melchizedek, king of Salem,
priest of the Most High God" (7:1), Hebrews comments, "He is
without father or mother or genealogy, having neither beginning of
days nor end of life, but resembling the Son of God he continues a
priest forever" (7:3).[8]

Some have understood this description as teaching that Melchizedek was a preincarnate appearance of the Son of God, a Christophany,
similar to the angel/messenger of the Lord, who was actually God

8   The Greek highlights the omissions by placing three adjectives in a row, without conjunctions (asyndeton): fatherless [*apatōr*], motherless [*amētōr*], genealogy-less [*agenealogētos*].

himself (Gen. 32:24–30; Ex. 3–4; see John 8:56–58).[9] There are good reasons, however, to doubt this interpretation. First, theophany/Christophany events in Old Testament narratives are brief in duration and distinguished by unusual phenomena that strike the recipients with awe so that they recognize that they have met the Lord. In Genesis 14, by contrast, Melchizedek is introduced as having a recognized political office (king of Salem, an ancient name for Jerusalem; see Ps. 76:2) and religious role (priest of God Most High). The text gives no indication that Abraham viewed him as anything other than human (although, as a priest, Melchizedek mediated between the patriarch and his God). Second, *Hebrews distinguishes Jesus from Melchizedek*, identifying Jesus as the priest who, by virtue of his faithful suffering, *has now become* "a high priest after the order of [fitting the pattern of] Melchizedek" (6:20; see 5:9–10). Melchizedek *was already* a priest when Abraham met him, but the Son *became* high priest when he assumed our human flesh and blood, endured temptation and suffering (2:14, 17–18; 5:8–10), offered himself as our sacrifice (10:5–10), took up his life again (13:20), and entered heaven on our behalf (10:24–26). Third, the statement that Melchizedek was "*made like [aphōmoiōmenos]*[10] the Son of God" draws a *distinction* between Melchizedek and the Son, even as it compares them. The "direction" of resemblance implies that the Son's eternal, divine life is the archetype, the original pattern after which Melchizedek was copied, as portrayed in Genesis.

So the terse summary in Hebrews—fatherless, motherless, genealogyless, birthless, and deathless—draws attention to the *silences* of the Genesis 14 record. In introducing the ancient priest-king who met Abraham, Moses *made no mention* of his father, mother, genealogy, birth, or death. These omissions make Melchizedek, *as Scripture speaks of him*, resemble the eternal life of the Son of God. Philip Edgcumbe Hughes comments,

9   Vern S. Poythress, *Theophany: A Biblical Theology of God's Appearing* (Wheaton, IL: Crossway, 2018), thoroughly explores this rich theme. See 257n1, where Poythress expresses agreement with my interpretation of Heb. 7:3.

10   The verb *aphōmoioō* appears only here in biblical Greek (LXX and NT). See the discussion of Heb. 7:3 in the entry on "ὅμοιος" and its cognates and compounds (including "ἀφομοιόω") in *NIDNTTE* 3:504.

It is not surprising that our author should regard the omission of any mention of parentage or posterity as remarkable. For one thing, in the early chapters of Genesis, in which genealogy is so prominent a feature . . . , Melchizedek is *the only personage* among the worshippers of the one true God *whose ancestry and descendants receive no mention.*[11]

If that mysterious but human ruler of ancient Salem, *whose origins and genealogy are unknown,* could be recognized by the great patriarch Abraham, recipient of God's promises, as a priestly mediator worthy to receive God's tithe and confer God's blessing, we should not be surprised to hear Psalm 110 announce an ever-living priest whose credentials transcend ancestry and are grounded, instead, in God's changeless oath. The author of Hebrews reads the Scriptures so reflectively that he can guide hearers to consider not only their affirmations and the significance of their historical contexts but also the implications of their Spirit-directed omissions.

A Close Reading of Psalm 110

Hebrews cites, interprets, and applies various Old Testament passages to demonstrate the superiority of Jesus to the angels who mediated the law (Heb. 1–2), to Moses who received that law (Heb. 3–4), to Aaron as high priest (Heb. 5–7), and to the old covenant with its sanctuary and sacrifices (Heb. 8–10).[12] Yet if we were to identify *a single scripture* that permeates and unifies this early Christian word of exhortation, it would be Psalm 110. George Wesley Buchanan fittingly described Hebrews as "a homiletical midrash based on Psalm 110"[13]—a sermon

---

11 Philip Edgcumbe Hughes, *A Commentary on the Epistle to the Hebrews* (Grand Rapids, MI: Eerdmans, 1977), 248 (emphasis added).

12 On the structuring of Hebrews's argument around specific Old Testament citations, see France, "The Writer of Hebrews," 260–72; Dennis E. Johnson, *Hebrews,* in *Hebrews–Revelation,* vol. 12 of *ESVEC,* ed. Iain M. Duguid, James M. Hamilton Jr., and Jay Sklar (Crossway, IL: Wheaton, 2018), 23 (table 1.1).

13 George Wesley Buchanan, *To the Hebrews,* Anchor Bible (Garden City, NY: Doubleday, 1972), xix.

("homiletical") that draws out ("midrash") the meaning and application of this psalm. Citations of or allusions to this psalm appear in Hebrews 1, 5, 6, 7, 8, 10, and 12.[14]

The author cites only Psalm 110:1 and 110:4, not directly mentioning the psalm's other verses, which elaborate on the victory over enemies (mentioned in 110:1) that God promises his enthroned king.

> The LORD says to my Lord:
>> "*Sit at my right hand,*
> until I make your enemies your footstool." (Ps. 110:1; cited or
>> alluded to in Heb. 1:3, 13; 12:2)

> The LORD has sworn
>> and will not change his mind,
> "You are *a priest forever*
>> after the order of Melchizedek." (Ps. 110:4: cited or alluded to in
>> Heb. 5:10; 6:20; 7:3, 11, 17, 20–22, 24, 26–28)

Hebrews sometimes treats 110:1 and 4 as individual texts, but eventually the author brings them together into a more complete portrait of the messianic priest-king:

- "a high priest . . . exalted above the heavens" (Heb. 7:26)
- "a high *priest . . . seated at the right hand* of the throne of the Majesty in heaven" (Heb. 8:1)
- "when Christ had offered for all time a single *sacrifice for sins*, he *sat down at the right hand* of God, waiting from that time until his enemies should be made a footstool for his feet" (Heb. 10:12–13)

These two texts share a common rhetorical structure, since both contain *words of direct address* spoken by "the LORD" (God the Father) to an individual who exercises both royal ("sit at my right hand")

---

14 Hebrews 2:17–3:1 and 4:14, which introduce Jesus's high priestly ministry, also display the thematic influence of Ps. 110:4.

and priestly ("priest forever") authority. In these verses we overhear the Father address the divine and messianic Son after he had become human (2:14), endured temptation (2:18), and made purification for sin by his death (1:3).

Psalm 110:1 is cited and alluded to throughout the New Testament. Wherever we read that Christ, after his death and resurrection, has ascended into heaven and taken his seat *at the right hand of God*, we encounter an allusion to Psalm 110:1 (e.g., Matt. 26:64 // Mark 14:62 // Luke 22:69; Acts 2:33–34; 5:31; 7:55–56; Rom. 8:34; Eph. 1:20; Col. 3:1; 1 Pet. 3:22). Paul alludes to Psalm 110:1 when he teaches that Christ, having been raised from the dead, must reign "until he has put all his enemies under his feet" (1 Cor. 15:25). The broad distribution of this verse across the spectrum of New Testament literature—Gospels, Acts, Pauline Epistles, and Petrine Epistles—is to be expected since Jesus applied it to himself more than once (in the Gospel texts cited above and in Matt. 22:41–45 // Mark 12:35–37 // Luke 20:41–44).[15]

For Hebrews, the relevance of Psalm 110:1 to the superiority of Jesus is threefold. First, Christ's enthronement at God's right hand entails *royal authority*, conferred in recognition of his priestly sacrifice for sin (Heb. 1:3). This theme Hebrews shares with other New Testament citations of the psalm. But the second and third inferences from Psalm 110:1 are unique to Hebrews, derived from the author's attention to other words in the psalm citation.

Second, the Messiah is now seated, by divine invitation, at the right hand "of the Majesty," which is "on high" (*en hypsēlois*, Heb. 1:3)—that is, "in heaven" (*en tois ouranois*, Heb. 8:1). He is carrying on his mediatorial ministry, therefore, *not on earth but in heaven*. The heavenly locale of this enthronement is significant for the author's articulation of Jesus's ministry as priest. The requirement of Levitical and Aaronic ancestry

---

15 Although Hebrews does not follow Jesus's lead in citing the first line of Ps. 110:1 ("The LORD says to my Lord") to show that David's messianic Son surpasses David in glory, Hebrews 1:5–13 does refer to Ps. 110:1, along with other texts (2 Sam. 7:14; Pss. 2:7; 45:6–7; 102:25–27), to demonstrate that Christ is greater than angels and the created cosmos, as we will see in the next chapter.

under the old covenant would disqualify Jesus, descended from Judah, from priestly service in the earthly tabernacle (Heb. 7:13–14; 8:4). But Psalm 110:1 speaks of a priest-king who serves in the very presence of God in *heaven,* the original sanctuary that was the template after which the earthly tent was copied (Heb. 8:5; see 9:11–12, 24).

Third, Hebrews draws attention to Christ's *seated posture* at God's right hand, which stands in contrast to the standing posture of the Levitical priests in the earthly tent:

> And every priest *stands daily* at his service, *offering repeatedly* the same sacrifices, which can never take away sins. But when Christ had offered for all time a single sacrifice for sins, *he sat down* at the right hand of God, waiting from that time until his enemies should be made a footstool for his feet. For *by a single offering he has perfected for all time* those who are being sanctified. (10:11–14)

Levitical priests had to stand and could not sit because their reconciling task was never done. By contrast, in Psalm 110 the Lord invites Jesus to take his seat: his atoning mission is completed through his once-for-all offering of himself.

The citation of Psalm 110:1 in Hebrews 1:13 and allusion to it in 10:13 include the announcement that the Messiah's enemies will be made a footstool for his feet. Since their subjugation is elaborated in Psalm 110:2–3, 5–7, we may wonder why these verses are neither cited nor alluded to in Hebrews. Hebrews 10:13 implies that the subjugation of enemies under the priest-king's feet is a future event for which he is presently "waiting." Only when that historical moment arrives will the Messiah "rule in the midst of [his] enemies" (Ps. 110:2), "shatter kings on the day of his wrath" (Ps. 110:5), and "execute judgment among the nations" (Ps. 110:6). Although Hebrews does orient believers toward the future, calling them to wait in hope for their priest-king's return to consummate their "salvation" (*eis sōtērian,* Heb. 9:28), our author's urgent concern is to ground his audience's faith firmly in Jesus's *present* heavenly ministry on their behalf. Thus, possibly because of his pastoral focus on his hearers' present needs, our author bypasses without comment the psalm's witness to Christ's future destruction of his enemies.[16]

In Hebrews 5:5–6, the author places the citation of Psalm 110:4 side by side with a citation of Psalm 2:7, which is the first Scripture in the catena of texts that demonstrates the Son's superiority to angels (Heb. 1:5–13). The author's point is that the Son, like Aaron, *did not seize* but *humbly received* priestly appointment by God's initiative:

> And no one takes this honor for himself, but only when called by God, just as Aaron was.
>
> So also Christ did not exalt himself to be made a high priest, but was appointed by him who said to him,
>
> "*You are* my Son,
>   today I have begotten you";
>
> as he says also in another place,
>
> "*You are* a priest forever,
>   after the order of Melchizedek." (5:4–6)

The opening words, "you are," are identical in English and semantically equivalent in Greek.[17] They bind Jesus's divine *sonship* with his *priestly appointment*, grounding both in God's address to Christ. The author

---

16 In 1 Cor. 15:25–27, Paul links the *underfoot* submission of all things to humankind in Ps. 8:6 with the *underfoot* subjugation of enemies in Ps. 110:1. The resurrection of Christ is the "firstfruits" that guarantees believers' future resurrection (1 Cor. 15:20, 23), so Christ's present reign secures the eventual subjugation of all his and our enemies, of which death is the last to be crushed underfoot. Hebrews 2:5–9 also sees in Ps. 8:4–6 the future submission of all creatures to humanity, which is "not yet" (Heb. 2:8) but is anticipated in the incarnate life trajectory of Jesus, who became briefly "lower than the angels" and has now been "crowned with glory and honor" (Heb. 2:9).

17 In Greek, the psalm citations open with *huios mou ei su*, "my Son are you" (Ps. 2:7), and *su (ei) hiereus*, "you (are) a priest" (Ps. 110:4). The verb *ei* ("you are") is present in the main LXX manuscripts of Ps. 110 and in a few NT manuscripts of Heb. 5:6, including the early Papyrus 46 (ca. AD 200).

goes on to describe the suffering that Jesus endured "in the days of his flesh" (5:7), his obedience (5:8), and his resultant appointment by God as "a high priest after the order of Melchizedek" (5:10).

After an extended exhortation (5:11–6:20), this motif is resumed and developed in Hebrews 7 where the psalm's mention of Melchizedek is linked to the other Old Testament text in which he appears (Gen. 14:18–20). That scripture reinforces the confluence of royal and priestly offices in this promised Messiah, since the ancient Melchizedek was both king of Salem and priest of the Most High God (Heb. 7:1). The patriarchal era predated the moment when, under the Mosaic covenant, God distributed *distinct* roles and spheres of authority to priests and to kings (Deut. 17:14–18:8; see 2 Chron. 26:16–21). By predicting a king whom the Lord would install as priest in Melchizedek's order, David reached back into the pre-Mosaic era to find the divinely ordained precedent for the future Messiah's multifaceted mission.

Further commentary on Psalm 110:4 in Hebrews 7:11–28 identifies two features that set apart this priest from the old covenant priestly order of Levi and Aaron. The first feature is the priest's *indestructible life* (7:11–19, 28). The royal priest in Melchizedek's order is installed as "priest *forever* [*eis ton aiōna*]" (7:17). He retains his office perpetually because of the power of his "indestructible life" (7:16). A genealogical criterion for identifying priestly successors, generation after generation, becomes unnecessary because this priest-king will never die. The Genesis portrait of the ancient Melchizedek, which makes no mention of an "end of life" (Heb. 7:3), finds fulfillment in the Christ who, having died once for others' sins, has been "made perfect forever [*eis ton aiōna*]" (7:28) and now "always [*pantote*] lives to make intercession for" his people (7:25).

The second feature that sets apart this priest is God's *irrevocable oath* (7:20–25, 28). Psalm 110:4 grounds the permanence of Christ's priesthood in God's unchangeable oath:

The LORD has sworn
and will not change his mind. (Ps. 110:4; see Heb. 7:20–21)

Aaron's descendants became high priests "without an oath" (Heb. 7:20), succeeding their fathers in accordance with the principle of genealogy. But "with an oath" (7:21), God invoked himself as witness and enforcer of his covenant commitment, sealing his word with his eternal, invincible life. God's solemn oath, addressed to Jesus the ever-living priest-king and "guarantor of a better covenant" (7:22), replaces ancestry as the means for certifying God's appointment to approach his holy presence on behalf of his guilty people.

Conclusion

As a "biblical expositor,"[18] the author to the Hebrews is a stimulating and sometimes surprising interpreter of the ancient Scriptures. Because he recognizes the Old Testament's divine origin, he gives careful attention not only to its specific words and ways of speaking but also to their placement in the history of redemption. Hebrews challenges us to hear God's word reflectively, attending closely to what the Scriptures include and exclude, to what they declare and what they imply. So Hebrews sharpens our hearing to listen to the testimonies of Moses, David, and others as they "testify to the things that were to be spoken later" (3:5), when God would speak at last in the Son.

---

18   France, "The Writer of Hebrews," 245.

4

The Divine-Human Mediator

Jesus, the Son of God.

HEBREWS 4:14

The Unchanging God Who Becomes Human

The person of Christ is among the deepest mysteries of the Christian faith. Since the fourth century AD, followers of Jesus have confessed,

> We believe . . . in One Lord Jesus Christ, the Son of God, begotten of the Father, Only-begotten, that is, from the substance of the Father; God from God, Light from Light, Very [True] God from Very [True] God, begotten not made, Consubstantial with the Father, by Whom all things were made, both things in heaven and things in earth; who for us men and for our salvation came down and was incarnate, was made man, suffered, and rose again the third day, ascended to heaven, and is coming to judge the living and the dead.[1]

---

1   Creed of Nicaea (AD 325), from a "Letter of Eusebius of Caesarea," in *A New Eusebius: Documents Illustrative of the History of the Church to A.D. 337*, ed. J. Stevenson (London: SPCK, 1957), 366. For the Greek text and a Latin translation, see "The Creed of Nicaea— Agreed at the Council in 325," Early Church Texts, accessed June 5, 2023, https://early churchtexts.com/. The Council of Constantinople (AD 381) introduced modifications, (including the insertion of "according to the Scriptures" in the second article concerning the Son, and additional affirmations in the third article concerning the Holy Spirit. The

The contrasts in this description of "*one* Lord Jesus Christ" are perplexing. This "Son of God" is no creature (contradicting the claim of the influential and dangerous Arius). He is "not made" but "begotten of the Father . . . from the substance of the Father," as truly God as the Father who begets him. The apostle Paul drew an unbridgeable contrast between God the Creator, on the one hand, and everything he has made, on the other (Rom. 1:19–25), and he categorized the Lord Jesus Christ on the Creator side of that great divide (Gal. 1:1). The Council of Nicaea heartily concurred.

Nevertheless, the Creed of Nicaea also affirms that this divine Son took on flesh and "was made man," experienced suffering, was raised from the dead, and ascended to heaven. How can God, who never changes (Mal. 3:6; James 1:17), *become* a man who "*increased* in wisdom and in stature" (Luke 2:52), experiencing the mutability that characterizes the created order (Heb. 1:10–12, cf. Ps. 102:25–27)? How can God incarnate, who *knows all things* (Ps. 147:5; Isa. 40:28; John 2:25; 21:17; Heb. 4:13), *acknowledge his ignorance* (Mark 13:32) and *learn obedience* through the things that he suffered (Heb. 5:8)? How can God, who cannot die (Rom. 1:23; 1 Tim. 1:17; 6:15–16), experience death (John 20:27–28)? How can this juxtaposition of infinite divine perfections and human limitations exist in a single person,[2] as Paul confesses: "For us

---

expanded form of the Nicene Creed (technically, Niceno-Constantinopolitan Creed) is typically confessed in Christian liturgies.

2   The Definition of the Council of Chalcedon (AD 451), a further clarification of the Nicene Christological confession, articulated more precisely the church's understanding of the Bible's teaching concerning the unity of Christ's person and the distinction between his divine and human natures: "We all with one voice confess our Lord Jesus Christ one and the same Son, the same perfect in Godhead, the same perfect in manhood, truly God and truly man, the same consisting of a reasonable soul and a body, of one substance with the Father as touching the Godhead, the same of one substance with us as touching the manhood, like us in all things apart from sin; begotten of the Father before the ages as touching the Godhead, the same in the last days, for us and for our salvation, born of the Virgin Mary, the *Theotocos* [*sic*], as touching the manhood, one and the same Christ, Son, Lord, Only-begotten, to be acknowledged in two natures, without confusion, without change, without division, without separation; the distinction of natures being in no way abolished because of the union, but rather the characteristic property of each nature being preserved, and concurring into one Person and one subsistence [ὑπόστασις], not as if Christ were parted or divided into two persons, but one and the same Son and only-begotten God, Word, Lord, Jesus Christ." *Creeds, Councils, and Controversies: Documents*

there is one God, the Father, from whom are all things and for whom we exist, and *one Lord, Jesus Christ*, through whom are all things and through whom we exist" (1 Cor. 8:6)?

Such paradoxes so boldly defy the limits of human reasoning that the New Testament's testimony—that Jesus is God's infinite, eternal Son and has entered space and time to take on a human nature—has been challenged in every generation. The centuries following the coming of Christ witnessed the rise of a host of attempts to "correct" the biblical witness—toning down either Jesus's deity, or his humanity, or his unity—in order to increase Christianity's plausibility to non-Christians and Christians alike. The Nicene Creed and other Christological confessions of the patristic period, however, were driven by the sense of obligation of faithful pastor-theologians to affirm *everything* that the Scriptures reveal about Christ the Lord. Those church fathers recognized that, as mystifying as this Redeemer is, the union of divine and human in his person is essential to his redemptive mission: "who *for us men and for our salvation* came down and was incarnate, was made man."[3]

The teaching of Hebrews about Christ draws together the truths of the Son's divine identity, his full embrace of human nature, and the redemptive purpose of his incarnation. Each of those themes is revealed in other New Testament documents, of course. But Hebrews stands out for the way it draws together these dimensions of the Son who became our brother (Heb. 2:12), our priest (2:17–18), and our covenant mediator (*mesitēs*, 8:6; 9:15; 12:24).

The Eternal Son of God

The prologue (Heb. 1:1–4) and following catena of Old Testament citations (1:5–14) affirm that the Son is superior to the angels. The author

---

Illustrative of the History of the Church A.D. 337–461, ed. J. Stevenson (New York: Seabury, 1966), 337. For the Greek text, see "The Chalcedonian Definition: Agreed at the Fourth Ecumenical Council at Chalcedon in 451," Early Church Texts, accessed June 5, 2023, https://earlychurchtexts.com/main/chalcedon/chalcedonian_definition.shtml.

3   Creed of Nicaea (AD 325), from a "Letter of Eusebius of Caesarea," 366. See this redemptive purpose also in the Definition of Chalcedon (echoing Nicaea), cited above.

has two purposes for drawing this contrast between the Son and the angels. First, he focuses on the Son's role in *revelation*. The texts that show the Son to be greater than the angels provide the basis for a "how much more" (*qal-ve-homer*) argument that underscores the seriousness with which hearers must attend to the message of salvation that the Son has spoken (2:1–4). Second, the author focuses on the Son's role in *redemption* (2:5–18). The priestly ministry of the Son of God is the sermon's main point (8:1), and that mission required him to share humanity's flesh and blood (2:14) to suffer and to endure temptation (2:18). Since priests are "chosen from among" human beings to act on their behalf (5:1), the Son "had to be made like his brothers in every respect, so that he might become a merciful and faithful high priest" (2:17). Therefore, "for us and for our salvation," as the creed says, the Son who transcends the angels became "for a little while . . . lower than the angels," as all humans are, in order to accomplish our rescue from guilt and death (2:9).

The epistle's prologue (1:1–4) introduces Christ's sonship from two perspectives. First, the Son is identified in terms of his *eternal, divine sonship* as the universe's heir, creator, and providential sustainer and as the unique display of God's glory (1:2–3). Then, we see the Son's redemptive mission in history, leading to his inauguration as *messianic Son*: "After making purification for sins" (his atoning death), "he sat down at the right hand" (his resurrection/ascension), having "inherited" the more excellent name "Son," signaling his superiority to the angels (1:3–5).

The Son's eternal deity is evident both from his engagement with the created universe and from his unique relationship with God himself. With respect to the created universe, our author begins with the end: God has appointed the Son "the heir [*klēronomos*] of all things," who is destined to own the entire creation (1:2). The language echoes Psalm 2, which will be cited as God's pronouncement of Christ's messianic sonship, when he "inherited" (*klēronomeō*) a more excellent name than that of the angels (1:4–5). In the psalm, after the Lord's decree,

You are my Son;
> today I have begotten you (Ps. 2:7),

comes his promise,

Ask of me,
> and I will make the nations your inheritance [LXX: *klēronomia*]"
>> (Ps. 2:8 CSB).

But Hebrews teaches that the Son inherits not only the earth's nations but *every created thing*. Such universal dominion is fitting since "through [the Son] also [God] created the world [or "the ages," *tous aiōnas*]" (Heb. 1:2). The referent of *tous aiōnas* is the physical, visible universe, as the parallel in Hebrews 11:3 shows, since both verses speak of God's original creation of the universe through his word. In Hebrews 1:2 the Son in whom God has now spoken is the one "through whom also he created the world [*epoiēsen tas aiōnas*]." Hebrews 11:3 similarly affirms, "By faith we understand that the universe was created [*katērtisthai tous aiōnas*] by the word of God, so that what is seen was not made out of things that are visible." In this couplet, "what is seen" in the second line corresponds to "the universe" (*tous aiōnas*) in the first.[4] Likewise, the statement in the prologue (1:2) is elaborated in Hebrews 1:10, where Psalm 102:25 is said to be addressed to the Son:

You, Lord, laid the foundation of the earth in the beginning,
> and the heavens are the work of your hands.

Our author knows that his audience is aware of the first sentence of the Torah: "In the beginning, God created the heavens and the earth"

---

4   The author's choice of *tous aiōnas* in Heb. 1:2 and 11:3 to refer to the created universe, rather than terms that he uses elsewhere—*oikoumenē* (1:6; 2:5), *kosmos* (10:5)—may be intended to suggest the connotation of the *temporal mutability* of the heavens and the earth, which is expressed in the citation of Ps. 102:25–27 in Heb. 1:10–12. The temporal sense of *aiōn*, especially in the frequent formula *eis ton aiōna*, "into the ages"* (or "forever"), dominates in Hebrews (1:8*; 5:6*; 6:5, 20*; 7:17*, 21*, 24*, 28*; 9:26; 13:8*, 21*).

(Gen. 1:1). The Son's presence and role in creation reveals his divine wisdom, power, and glory.

The Son is not only the universe's Creator and the heir for whom it is destined in the end, but he is also the sovereign sustainer of its very existence: "He upholds the universe [ta panta, "all things"] by the word of his power" (Heb. 1:3). Unlike angels, who are finite servants dependent on their Creator for life, the Son is the divine Creator, providential sustainer, and rightful possessor of all things.

The reference in Hebrews to the Son's *agency in creation* as revealing his eternal deity resonates with the witness of other New Testament authors. The Fourth Gospel begins:

> In the beginning was the Word, and the Word was with God, and *the Word was God.* . . . *All things were made through him,* and without him was not any thing made that was made. . . . And the Word became flesh and dwelt among us, and we have seen his glory, glory as of the only Son from the Father, full of grace and truth. (John 1:1, 3, 14)

Paul describes God's "beloved Son" (Col. 1:13) as

> the image of the invisible God, the firstborn of all creation. For *by him all things were created*, in heaven and on earth, visible and invisible, whether thrones or dominions or rulers or authorities—*all things were created through him and for him.* And he is before all things, and in him *all things hold together.* (Col. 1:15–17)

The Son is the preeminent heir, the firstborn[5] to whom all created things belong, for everything was created "for [eis] him" (Col. 1:16), destined to be his possession. Just as Hebrews extols the Son who "upholds"

---

5 "Firstborn" (*prōtotokos*) identifies the Son, not as a first creature but rather as *the preeminent heir* to whom the entire creation belongs by the Father's appointment. See the discussion below on the Old Testament background of the use of "firstborn" in Heb. 1:6. In contrast, the New World Translation of Jehovah's Witnesses views "firstborn" as teaching that the Son is a creature, not the Creator. Note the comment on Col. 1:16 at their website: "Jesus was Jehovah's firstborn Son and the only one created directly by God.

(*pherō*) all things by the word of his power (Heb. 1:3), so also Paul affirms that in him all things "hold together" (*synistēmi*) (Col. 1:17). His providential power and sovereign control sustain the existence and interconnectedness of all that he has made.

Two descriptions articulate the Son's unique relationship to God the Father: "the radiance [*apaugasma*] of the glory of God and the exact imprint [*charactēr*] of his nature" (Heb. 1:3). Both terms are rare in ancient Greek literature prior to the New Testament, and neither appears elsewhere in the New Testament.[6] Together, these terms identify Jesus as the visibly resplendent and entirely accurate display of the invisible God himself. William Lane comments, "[The author] used the word [*charactēr*] to convey as emphatically as he could his conviction that in Jesus Christ there had been provided a perfect, visible expression of the reality of God."[7] Again, the author's Christological confession of the Son's relationship to God the Father resonates with the testimony of the broader New Testament:

And the Word became flesh and dwelt among us, and *we have seen his glory*, glory as of the only Son from the Father, full of grace and truth. (John 1:14)

Jesus said, . . . "Whoever has seen me has seen the Father." (John 14:9)

For God, who said, "Let light shine out of darkness," has shone in our hearts to give *the light of the knowledge of the glory of God* in the face of Jesus Christ. (2 Cor. 4:6)

When this eternal Son enters history and humanity, coming to "share in flesh and blood" with his "children" (Heb. 2:14)—when, in Paul's terms, "the whole fullness of deity dwells bodily" in Jesus (Col. 2:9)—we hear

---

(Heb 1:6; see study notes on Joh[n] 1:14 and Col 1:15.)." See "Letter to the Colossians 1:1–29," Jehovah's Witnesses, accessed June 7, 2023, https://www.jw.org/.

6 The LXX book Wisdom of Solomon describes wisdom as the "radiance [*apaugasma*] of eternal light" (Wis 7:26). In Lev. 13:28 LXX "exact imprint" (*charactēr*) describes a scar left by a burn.

7 William L. Lane, *Hebrews 1–8*, WBC 47A (Dallas: Word, 1991), 13.

God's voice addressing us through a spokesman whose glory transcends both human prophets and holy angels (Heb. 2:1, 4). Better yet, we meet a divine-human mediator who achieves our eternal redemption (9:12) and draws us close to God (4:14–16; 7:22; 8:6; 12:24). The string of Old Testament quotations in Hebrews 1:5–13 elaborates the prologue's announcement of this eternal divine sonship. Psalm 102:25–27 (Heb. 1:10–12) illustrates the divine Son's role in the creation of the universe:

> You, Lord,[8] laid the foundation of the earth in the beginning,
>   and the heavens are the work of your hands. (Heb. 1:10)

God the Father addresses the Son with the divine name, "Lord," and affirms his preincarnate agency in the act of creation. This Scripture sets the Son apart from the earth and the heavens and all "the work of your hands," affirming *his immutability* in contrast to their transience:

> they will perish, but you remain [*diamenō*];
>   they will all wear out like a garment,
> like a robe you will roll them up,
>   like a garment they will be changed.
> But you are the same [*ho autos*],
>   and your years will have no end. (1:11–12)

This distinction between the changeless Creator and his mutable creation is significant for the author's theological argument. The Son's divine immutability comes to expression in his everlasting tenure in priestly ministry. By virtue of his "indestructible [*akatalytos*] life"[9] (7:17), he "holds his priesthood permanently, because he continues

8 Hebrews follows the reading of the Septuagint (Ps. 101:26 LXX), which inserts "Lord" (*kyrios*) to specify the addressee as Israel's covenant God. Although the MT lacks a title at this point, Yahweh appears as a vocative address earlier in the psalm (Ps. 102:1, 13 MT).

9 *Akatalytos*, which appears only here in the New Testament, means impervious to being "destroyed" (*katalyō*), unlike, for instance, the temple in Jerusalem (Matt. 24:2) and our human bodies (2 Cor. 5:1).

[*menō*] forever" (7:24). Later, the author's reminder that, though the congregation's human leaders have passed away (13:7), "Jesus Christ is the same [*ho autos*] yesterday and today and forever" (13:8), overtly echoes his citation of Psalm 102.

The created order, however, is wearing out like frayed clothing, and this tendency toward decomposition applies also to the old covenant's sanctuary, the tent pitched by people and crafted by human hands, which was destined by God for obsolescence and replacement by the true, original, heavenly sanctuary that Christ has entered on our behalf (8:2, 13; 9:1–11, 24). Looking toward the future, Hebrews anticipates the moment when God's voice will shake "not only the earth but also the heavens," and all "things that have been made" will be removed (12:26–27). At that time only God's unshakable kingdom, and its blessed heirs, will remain (12:27–28).

The Messianic Son of God

The prologue to Hebrews also introduces Christ as the messianic Son, who offered himself in death and consequently has "become . . . superior to angels" and "has inherited" the name that is "more excellent than theirs" (1:4). Both verbs—"having become" (*genomenos*) and "has inherited" (*keklēronomēken*)—describe a *transition* that the Son underwent *as a result of* his self-sacrifice. In other words, the prologue affirms not only the divine Son's eternal preexistence and identity as the perfect display of God's glory (1:2–3) but also his incarnate mission to purify others' sins (1:3) and his resultant exaltation (1:3–4). Immediately after this announcement, the author introduces the first text in a catena of Old Testament quotations (Ps. 2:7) with a rhetorical question:

For to which of the angels did God ever say,

"You are my Son,
    today I have begotten you"? (Heb. 1:5)[10]

---

10 The series concludes with Ps. 110:1, introduced by the same rhetorical question: "And to which of the angels has he ever said . . . ?" (Heb. 1:13). This rhetorical question signals

The conjunction "for" (*gar*) in 1:5 shows that the "more excellent" name (1:4) is "Son." Philip E. Hughes observes,

> It is true, of course, that by virtue of his eternal Sonship he has an eternal inheritance and possesses a name which is eternally supreme. ... But our author is speaking at this point of something other than this: the Son who for our redemption humbled himself for a little while to a position lower than the angels has by his ensuing exaltation *become* superior to the angels (2:9 below), and in so doing has achieved and retains the inheritance of a name which is more superior than theirs. Once more, then, the reference is to the Son as Mediator and to the sequence of his humiliation and glorification as, so to speak, historical events.[11]

The author's identification of the Messiah's *exaltation* (the resurrection-ascension-enthronement complex) as the historic moment when Psalm 2:7 found fulfillment agrees with other New Testament witnesses. On the day of Pentecost, Peter proclaimed that God, by raising Jesus from the dead (fulfilling Ps. 16:8–11) and seating him at his right hand (fulfilling Ps. 110:1), "made him both Lord and Christ, this Jesus whom you crucified" (Acts 2:36; see Acts 2:25–36). Alongside the title "Lord" from Ps. 110:1, Peter puts the title "Christ" ("Anointed," "Messiah"), alluding to Yahweh's address to his Christ (Ps. 2:2, cf. 2:7). Paul instructs a synagogue congregation,

> God raised him from the dead, and for many days he appeared to those who had come up with him from Galilee to Jerusalem, who are now his witnesses to the people. And we bring you the good news that what God promised to the fathers, this he *has fulfilled* to us their children *by raising Jesus*, as also it is written in the second Psalm,

---

an inclusio that marks the catena's boundaries and emphasizes the Son's unique exalted status in contrast to angels.

11   Philip Edgcumbe Hughes, *A Commentary on the Epistle to the Hebrews* (Grand Rapids, MI: Eerdmans, 1977), 50–51 (emphasis in original).

"You are my Son,
> today I have begotten you." (Acts 13:30–33)

It was Jesus's *resurrection* that fulfilled the Lord's address to his anointed one in Psalm 2:7: "Today I have begotten you." The one who has *eternally* been God's Son—Creator, sustainer, radiance of the Father's glory—now, at a moment in history, has become superior to angels and inherited the name "Son" at his exaltation (his resurrection, ascension, and heavenly enthronement). By using the title "Son" in two distinct senses in his prologue, our author anticipates not only his case for the Son's superiority to angels (1:5–13) but also the startling truth that this Son "for a little while was made lower than the angels" and subsequently "crowned with glory and honor" (2:9).[12]

Two Old Testament quotations in the series that follows the prologue (1:5–13) confirm its Christological portrait of Jesus as both divine Son and messianic Son. The third quotation in the catena expresses God's demand that angels bow before the superior glory of his "firstborn" Son: "Let all God's angels worship him" (1:6). The source of this citation is

---

12 James D. G. Dunn, *Christology in the Making: A New Testament Inquiry into the Origins of the Doctrine of the Incarnation* (Philadelphia: Westminster, 1980), 52–53, attributes the two senses of sonship in Heb. 1:2–5 ("this odd juxtaposition of seemingly contradictory themes") to "the unique synthesis of Platonic and Hebraic worldviews, or more precisely Platonic cosmology and Judaeo-Christian eschatology, which this letter achieves." He suggests "that *the awkward tensions in [the author's] presentation of Christ are the result of his merging these two worldviews*" (emphasis in original). Contrary to Dunn, those who discern in the New Testament documents an early high Christology trace the origin of the paradoxical affirmation of Christ's eternal deity and genuine humanity not to an evolutionary merger of intellectual worldviews but rather to the apostles' direct experience of the words and works of Jesus himself, which formed the primitive church's worship of Jesus in the decades immediately following his death and resurrection. See, e.g., R. T. France, "The Worship of Jesus: A Neglected Factor in Christological Debate?," in *Christ the Lord: Studies in Christology Presented to Donald Guthrie*, ed. Harold H. Rowdon (Downers Grove, IL: InterVarsity Press, 1982), 17–36. See also the works of such scholars as Martin Hengel, *The Son of God: The Origin of Christology and the History of Jewish-Hellenistic Religion* (Philadelphia: Fortress, 1976); Larry Hurtado, *One God One Lord: Early Christian Devotion and Ancient Jewish Monotheism*, 2nd ed. (New York: T&T Clark, 1988); and Richard Bauckham, *God Crucified: Monotheism and Christology in the New Testament* (Grand Rapids, MI: Eerdmans, 1999).

uncertain, since the wording resembles, but does not reproduce, two Septuagint passages, both of which vary from the MT (Deut. 32:43 LXX; Ps. 96:7 LXX [97:7 MT]).[13]

In both, God's angels are commanded to worship the Lord himself. The object of their worship can only be the Creator of heaven and earth, the God of Israel, who tolerates no rivals (Ex. 20:1–3: Deut. 6:4–5, 13–15; see Matt. 4:10; Rev. 22:8–10). In the introduction to this citation ("Let all God's angels worship him")—"again,[14] *when* he brings his firstborn (*prōtotokos*) into the world, he says" (Heb. 1:6)—the author identifies the Son as the divine object of angelic worship. This introduction indicates a moment in time when God commands angels to worship his "firstborn." That moment is when God brings the Son "into the world [*oikoumenē*]." But this time reference is debatable. If "the world" is this earth *in contrast to heaven*, the reference could be to the angelic worship associated with the incarnation (Luke 2:8–25). But when Hebrews later describes the incarnation, when Christ "came into the world" to do God's will in death, the author uses a different Greek word for "world" (*kosmos*) (Heb. 10:5). The term used here reappears only in "the world [*oikoumenē*] to come" (Heb. 2:5), a reference to *the eschatological future* when humans will be "crowned with glory and honor." God brought Jesus into that "world to come" at *his resurrection/ascension,* when he inherited the title "Son" as incarnate Messiah. That was the moment he was "vindicated by the Spirit, seen by angels," and "taken up in glory" (1 Tim. 3:16). Having embraced humankind's humble status, becoming briefly "lower than angels," the Son has "*become* . . . superior to angels" (Heb. 1:4), so God commands all angels to worship this incarnate and exalted Son (cf. Rev. 5:8–14).

13 Deuteronomy 32:43 LXX contains lines absent from the MT (though they are in the Qumran Deuteronomy scroll): "Let all God's sons *worship him.* . . . Let all *God's angels* grow strong in him" (my translation). Psalm 96:7 LXX reads, "Worship him, all his angels" (my translation), whereas the MT (97:7) says, "Worship him, all gods."

14 Just as "again" (*palin*) links Ps. 2:7 and 2 Sam. 7:14 (Heb. 1:5) so in Heb. 1:6 "again" ties a third citation to the previous two. The adverb "again" is *not* to be tied to the verb "he brings," as though God's command to angels takes place at Christ's *second coming* into the world.

His title "firstborn" (*prōtotokos*) highlights his supremacy as heir and alludes to Psalm 89:

> I have found David, my servant;
> with my holy oil I have anointed him.
> . . . .
> He shall cry to me, "You are my Father,
> my God, and the Rock of my salvation."
> And I will make him the *firstborn* [*prōtotokos*],
> *the highest of the kings of the earth.*
> My steadfast love I will keep for him forever,
> and my covenant will stand firm for him. (Ps. 89:20, 26–28
> [88:21, 27–29 LXX])

Like Psalm 2, this psalm is rooted in God's covenant promise to establish David's royal dynasty in perpetuity, recorded in 2 Samuel 7:14 (cited in Heb. 1:5). Jesus is the royal Son descended from David (Luke 1:30–33; Rom. 1:3), so he is the supreme ruler to whom all earth's kings must submit (Ps. 2:2, 10–12) and whom all heaven's angels must worship.

The fifth Old Testament text in the catena (Heb. 1:8–9) is Psalm 45:6–7 (44:7–8 LXX), often considered a wedding song for a Davidic king. The king is addressed as God, while God is also the divine sovereign who has anointed the king:

> Your throne, *O God*, is forever and ever,
> the scepter of uprightness is the scepter of your kingdom.
> You have loved righteousness and hated wickedness;
> therefore *God, your God*, has *anointed* [*chriō*] you
> with the oil of gladness beyond your companions. (Heb. 1:8–9)

The Son is a *human* king who has been anointed by his God (as we also heard in Ps. 89:20 [88:21 LXX]). He is the "Anointed" (*christos*) whom God has set as King "on Zion, my holy hill" and has called "my

Son" (Ps. 2:2, 6–7 LXX). His reign displays his love of "righteous-ness" (*dikaiosynē*) (Heb. 1:9), so he is the perfect exemplar of ancient Melchizedek's name, "king of righteousness" (*basileus dikaiosynēs*) (7:2). Although his reign is endless—his throne "is forever and ever" (1:8)—his royal anointing, which set him apart from his companions, is the reward of his obedience (1:9). So Psalm 45 (Ps. 44 LXX) traces the messianic Son's trajectory from righteous obedience to royal en-thronement, which Hebrews observes in Jesus (Heb. 1:3–4; 5:8–10; 7:28–8:1; 9:24–28; 10:12–14; 12:2).

This Son, this righteous human king, is nevertheless addressed *by* God *as* God: "Your throne, O God, is forever and ever" (1:8, citing Ps. 44:7 LXX). Major translations of the psalm's original Hebrew interpret "God" as a title directly addressed to the king (CSB, ESV, NASB, NIV). On the one hand, the direct address, "O God," is so jarring that some translations offer readings of Psalm 45:6 that avoid the idea that the king is *addressed as God*: "Your *divine* throne endures forever and ever" (RSV);[15] "your throne is *like God's* throne, eternal" (NEB); "your throne is *God's throne*, ever and always" (MSG). On the other hand, Old Tes-tament scholar Derek Kidner, while acknowledging "the astonishing words addressed to the king in verses 6 and 7," insists,

> But the Hebrew resists any softening here, and it is the New Testa-ment, not the new versions, which does justice when it uses it to prove the superiority of God's Son to the very angels (Heb. 1:8f.). . . . Verse 7 distinguishes between *God, your God*, and the king who has been addressed as "God" in verse 6. This paradox is consistent with the incarnation, but mystifying in any other context. It is an example of Old Testament language bursting its banks, to demand a more than human fulfilment (as did Ps. 110:1, according to our Lord).[16]

---

15 Although the RSV had "divine throne" with marginal alternatives ("Your throne is a throne of God" or "Thy throne, O God"), the NRSV rendered it as "your throne, O God, endures forever and ever."

16 Derek Kidner, *Psalms 1–72: Introduction and Commentary*, TOTC (Downers Grove, IL: InterVarsity Press, 1973), 172 (emphasis in original).

Psalm 45 is a divine witness, imparted "long ago" through "the prophets" (Heb. 1:1), to this beautiful mystery: the divine Son whom God calls "God" has entered humanity and David's royal line as the messianic Son. His love of righteousness has been rewarded by exaltation to the throne that "is forever and ever" (Heb. 1:8, citing Ps. 45:6) at God's "right hand" (Heb. 1:13, citing Ps. 110:1).

Son of Man

The other indispensable dimension of the Christology of Hebrews is the genuine and complete *humanity* of the new covenant's mediator, our "great high priest" (2:5–18 with 4:14–5:10). Just as the rhetorical questions in 1:5 and 1:13 form an inclusio to the catena that establishes the Son's superiority to angels, so also the exploration of the Son's humanity is enveloped by another inclusio: "not (to) angels" (2:5, 16). These terms imply contrasting affirmations:

- God subjected the world to come "not to angels" (2:5) but to *man* who—though made briefly "lower than the angels"—is to be crowned with "glory and honor" with all things in subjection "under his feet" (2:7–8).
- God helps "not angels" but "the offspring of Abraham" (2:16).

These framing statements focus our attention on God's personal care for *human beings*, specifically for those who, like their father Abraham, inherit God's promises of grace "through faith and patience" (6:12; see 6:12–20; 11:8–19).

The discussion of Christ's humanity begins with Psalm 8:4–6 (Heb. 2:5–8). Our author reads the psalm's celebration of humankind's dignity and dominion not as a retrospective on the past nor as an idealization of the present but rather as a forecast of the future—a glimpse of "the world [*oikoumenē*] to come," which "we do not yet see" in our experience (2:5, 8). The psalm's portrait of humanity's humble status ("lower than the angels") alongside our royal dignity ("crowned with glory and honor") summarizes two *successive stages in God's redemptive-historical timeline* for his human image bearers: *first* made lower than the angels and *then* crowned with glory and honor. Although the Greek adverbial construction *brachy ti* ("a little") could refer to a minimal *degree* in distance or status, the ESV correctly interprets *brachy ti* as a minimal *duration*, "a little while."[17]

Our author first cites Psalm 8 as revealing the destiny of dominion to be enjoyed by *human beings in general* in the world to come. Yet the destination of the historical trajectory that the psalm traces—from "a little lower" to "glory and honor" and dominion—is "not yet" visible in human experience generally (2:7–8). Nevertheless, we do "see" one man (2:9)—one son of man[18]—whose life story has already passed through humiliation and into glory. He is introduced in terms drawn from the psalm: "We see him who for a little while was made lower than the angels" (2:9). Then we read his human name, Jesus. His story is resumed in the psalm's words: "crowned with glory and honor" (2:9). In showing how Jesus fits the pattern of the psalm, our author injects the redemptive purpose for which the Son became briefly lower than angels. It was "because of the suffering of death, so that by the grace of God he might taste death for everyone," that Jesus first endured humiliation before he experienced exaltation (2:9). By Christ's suffering, God leads "many sons to glory" (2:10), the glory with which Jesus is already crowned.

17 See footnote 21 on p. 57 for my discussion of *brachy* in chap. 2.

18 In the Gospels, Jesus's preference for the title "Son of Man" in referring to himself typically reflects the background of the visions in Dan. 7. In those visions, four evil beasts appear, and then the heavenly court of the Ancient of Days appears. Into that divine court "one like a son of man" (Dan. 7:13)—representing "the saints of the Most High" (Dan. 7:18)—enters on heaven's clouds to receive worldwide and eternal dominion in an indestructible kingdom. Although Ps. 8 (and Hebrews, citing the psalm) uses "son of man" in synonymous parallelism with "man" in the previous line, the psalm and Daniel's vision share Adamic overtones that anticipate the restoration of human dominion, forfeited by Adam, through the obedience of a second "Adam," the coming representative head of a redeemed humanity. Unlike Paul (Rom. 5:12–21; 1 Cor. 15:21–22), Hebrews does not *explicitly* compare Adam's role and Christ's (as covenant representatives acting on behalf of others) nor contrast their performance in that role (Adam's transgression brings death; Christ's obedience brings life). Nevertheless, thematically Hebrews comes close to Paul's Adam Christology.

As we will see in the next chapter, Hebrews 2:10–18 not only affirms the humanity of Jesus but also explains how his incarnation qualified him to be our "merciful and faithful high priest" (2:17). At this point, we note the author's insistence that the divine Son fully embraced human nature with its weakness and vulnerability to harm and death:

- "Since therefore the children share in flesh and blood, *he himself likewise partook of the same things*" (2:14).
- "Therefore he had to be *made like his brothers in every respect*, so that he might become a merciful and faithful high priest in the service of God" (2:17).
- "For because *he himself has suffered when tempted*, he is able to help *those who are being tempted*" (2:18).

The Son's incarnation involves not only receiving a physical body of "flesh and blood" (2:14; see 10:5–10) but also sharing humans' psychological experience (intellectual, affectional, emotional, spiritual). Because the Son assumed to himself a complete human nature, he experienced a process of maturation through trials (5:8), and his sufferings posed real temptations to sin (2:18; 4:15; see Matt. 4:1–11; Luke 4:1–13). The Gospels give glimpses of this inner dimension of the incarnate Son's humanity: his growth in wisdom (Luke 2:52), his sorrow and outrage over death (John 11:33, 35, 38), and his anguish at the daunting prospect of enduring God's wrath (Matt. 26:36–46; Luke 12:50; John 12:27–28; 13:21). Hebrews reflects the Gospels' testimony: "In the days of his flesh, Jesus offered up prayers and supplications, with loud cries and tears, to him who was able to save him from death, and he was heard because of his reverence. Although he was a son, he learned obedience through what he suffered" (Heb. 5:7–8). The mention of "prayers and supplications, with loud cries and tears" alludes to the emotional intensity of Christ's experience in Gethsemane, when he became "sorrowful and troubled" (Matt. 26:37). The description of God in Hebrews as the one who "was able to save him from death" sums up the content of Jesus's desperate plea: "My Father, if it be possible, let this cup [of wrath and death] pass from me" (Matt. 26:39). Hebrews asserts that because of his reverence, Jesus "was heard" (Heb. 5:7)—that is, his petition was granted, as when God "heard" suffering psalmists' prayers *and rescued them* (e.g., Pss. 6:9; 18:6; 22:24; 116:1). His "reverence" was expressed in his submission to God's will: "nevertheless, not as I will, but as you will" (Matt. 26:39). But was Jesus's plea "heard" by God? In the end, God answered, not by sparing him from death (*ek thanatou*)—in fact, that death was the purpose of his incarnation (Heb. 2:9–10; 10:5–10). Rather, God answered by bringing him again *out from the* dead ones (*ek nekrōn*) through resurrection (13:20). Luke Timothy Johnson observes that God's answer came, "not by Jesus escaping death, or the fear of death, but by his transcending death through his resurrection and exaltation to God's right hand."[19]

The Son's embrace of human nature and experience is expressed in the statement, "Although being Son, from what he suffered [*epathen*] he learned [*emathen*] obedience, and, having been perfected, he became to those who obey him the source of eternal salvation" (Heb. 5:8–9, my translation). The statement is surprising. As the opening "although" (*kaiper*)[20] signals, there is something incongruous about Jesus's identity as "Son," on the one hand, and his learning obedience through suffering, on the other. Later, Hebrews will reason from Proverbs 3:11–12 and normal human experience that *painful discipline* demonstrates God's fatherly love for his sons (Heb. 12:5–11). If that logic were operative in Hebrews 5:8, we would expect the author to say, "*Because* he was a Son," he learned obedience through suffering. Yet, as James Moffatt observes,

> Here the remarkable thing is that Jesus had to suffer, not because but although he was *huios*, which shows that Jesus is Son in a unique sense; as applied to Jesus *huios* [Son] means something special. As

19 Luke Timothy Johnson, *Hebrews: A Commentary*, NTL (Louisville: Westminster John Knox, 2006), 146.

20 Compare other uses of *kaiper* in Hebrews to convey counterintuitive concepts: Heb. 7:5; 12:17.

divine *huios* in the sense of 1:1f., it might have been expected that he would be exempt from such a discipline.[21]

Only by taking on our flesh and blood could the divine Son, who remains "the same" (1:12), share our experience of learning obedience through suffering.

We may be surprised to read that the Son "learned obedience" and became "perfected." In our experience, "learning obedience" involves a disciplinary process by which *moral flaws are corrected* by painful discipline (12:5–11). But with respect to Jesus, our author denies Jesus's need to progress out of a state of sinful guilt and into a state of holy purity. He was "without sin" (4:15) and "holy, innocent, unstained, separated from sinners" (7:26–27). Yet the author uses a memorable play on words, pairing "learned" with "suffered," to sum up the reality of the incarnate Son's lifelong experience of facing *escalating temptations* to doubt and disobey the Father and of resisting every invitation to unbelief and sin. F. F. Bruce explains,

> As we are told later (10:7), he announced his dedication to doing God's will at his coming into the world. He set out from the start on the path of obedience to God, and *learned by the sufferings* that came his way in consequence *just what obedience to God involved in practice* in the conditions of human life on earth.[22]

In the same vein, Hugh Montefiore comments, "The greater the test, the more profound obedience it evoked. Thus the Son learnt full obedience

---

21 James Moffatt, *A Critical and Exegetical Commentary on the Epistle to the Hebrews*, ICC (Edinburgh: T&T Clark, 1924), 66.

22 F. F. Bruce, *The Epistle to the Hebrews*, NICNT, rev. ed. (Grands Rapids, MI: Eerdmans, 1990), 131(emphasis added). Geerhardus Vos observes, " 'Learning' is not here equivalent to acquiring what was not previously there in principle, far less to acquiring that of which the opposite was previously there. . . . 'Learning' simply means to bring out into the conscious experience of action, that which is present as an avowed principle antecedent to the action." Geerhardus Vos, "The Priesthood of Christ in the Epistle to the Hebrews," in *Redemptive History and Biblical Interpretation: The Shorter Writings of Geerhardus Vos*, ed. Richard B. Gaffin Jr. (Phillipsburg, NJ: P&R, 1980), 147.

in the only way possible in an incarnate life, through submission to the will of God in a situation of ultimate concern and under pressure of emotional shock and physical distress."[23] As we will see in the next chapter, for Hebrews the concept of being "perfected" (*teleioō*) refers not to a *process* of moral improvement but to an *event* that imparts access to approach God in his holy sanctuary. For sinful humans, such a "perfecting" event must entail forgiveness of sins and cleansing of conscience (10:1, 14). For Jesus himself, however, his "being made perfect" (2:10; 5:9; 7:28) is equivalent to his being "appointed priest forever," his induction into priestly office through his obedience and death. Parallel aorist passive participles—"having been perfected" (*teleiōtheis*) and "having been appointed" (*prosagoreutheis*) by God as high priest—describe Jesus's priestly consecration (perfection) and installation in complementary terms (5:9–10).

Conclusion

The great Christological motifs revealed in the rest of the Scripture converge in Hebrews. The Son's *eternal deity* and his role as Creator of the universe are taught in John 1, Colossians 1, and Hebrews 1. The Son's *true humanity*—which entailed his growth and learning, weakness and suffering, temptation and obedience—appear in the four Gospels and in Hebrews 2, 4, and 5. The God-man's *messianic sonship*, in which he followed the path of humiliation to glory in order to achieve our redemption, is presented in Jesus's own interpretation of the Old Testament (Luke 24), in the sermons of Acts, in Romans and other Pauline Epistles, and in Hebrews 1, 2, 5, 7, 10, 13.

Hebrews devotes such attention to the *identity* of the Christ in order to show us that just such a Redeemer is God's "fitting" (*prepō*) solution to our desperate spiritual need (2:10; 7:26). We need a priest who has unhindered access to God but who also identifies with our human frailty and can sympathize with our weakness. We need an intercessor who has experienced the temptations that defeat us but who resisted

23 Hugh Montefiore, *The Epistle to the Hebrews*, HNTC (San Francisco: Harper and Row, 1964), 99–100.

temptation's allure from birth to his sacrificial death on our behalf. We need a mediator who lives forever, never needing a successor, whose indestructible life secures our salvation to the uttermost. By sending his Son into this sin-stained world to participate in humanity and to deal the death blow to death itself, God has shown himself to be the ever-faithful helper to the offspring of Abraham who trust his promises.

5

Jesus's Priestly Qualifications and Tenure

A merciful and faithful high priest.

HEBREWS 2:17

We Need a Priest

Jesus's priesthood is the main theme of this sermon to the Hebrew Christians: "Now the point [*kephalaion*][1] in what we are saying is this: we have such a high priest, one who is seated at the right hand of the throne of the Majesty in heaven" (Heb. 8:1). This statement marks the pivotal transition in the sermon's longest section, an extended discussion of Christ's priesthood, which is superior to that of Aaron (4:14–10:25). That section addresses, first, the issue of *priestly qualification* to enter God's presence on behalf of others (4:14–7:28). Then, after the *kephalaion* summary itself, the discourse pivots to Christ's *priestly ministry*, including the covenant that he mediates, the sanctuary in which he serves, and the sacrifice that he has offered (8:2–10:25).

---

[1] In contexts related to literary composition, the Greek term *kephalaion* refers to a summation or central thought (Dan. 7:1 LXX; Heb. 8:1). In mathematical contexts, it means a total amount, either of persons (Num. 4:2; 31:49 LXX) or of material goods (Lev. 6:4 [5:24 MT and LXX]; Num. 5:7; 31:26; Acts 22:28).

The author's Jewish-Christian audience understood their need for a priestly mediator to intervene on their behalf in God's sanctuary. Ancient Israelites and early Christians needed no persuasion to experience fear over the prospect of drawing near to the holy, sovereign Creator, who is a "consuming fire," ablaze with zeal for his own glory and lethally dangerous to sin-defiled humans (Heb. 12:29; cf. Deut. 4:24; Isa. 33:14). Moderns and postmoderns may dismiss the fear of God as archaic, primitive, and demeaning to human dignity. The Israelites at Mount Sinai and first-century Jesus followers knew better.

The institution of priesthood is God's answer to a dilemma that sinful human beings cannot solve for themselves: we cannot live *apart from* communion with the God who gives and sustains life; but, stained as we are by sin, we cannot survive *close to* his consuming holiness, either. The instinct of our first parents was right: they hid in shame and fear at the sound of God's approach (Gen. 3:7–8). Their rebellion had transformed the nearness of their generous and good Creator from an occasion of joy into one of mortal danger.

Israel's experience in the wilderness dramatized this excruciating dilemma. From the foot of Sinai, the Israelites looked up to see a cloud of smoke and fiery lightning bolts on the mountaintop, heard crashing thunder and trumpet blasts, and felt the ground shudder under their feet (Ex. 19:16–20; Heb. 12:18–20, 26). Sensing their peril from the Lord's approach, they implored Moses, "You speak to us, and we will listen; but do not let God speak to us, lest we die" (Ex. 20:19). Their terror was well placed. In fact, the Lord had already demanded that, though they had been ritually consecrated, the Israelites should not ascend the mountain. Moses alone could approach God on their behalf (Ex. 19:10–15). So "the people stood far off, while Moses drew near to the thick darkness where God was" (Ex. 20:21). They needed God's word, for "man lives by every word that comes from the mouth of the Lord" (Deut. 8:3). Yet to have the Lord address them directly would destroy them. So Moses entered God's fiery cloud to receive the law and emerged to read it to the people. They responded, "All that the Lord has spoken we will do, and we will be obedient" (Ex. 24:7), so the covenant was ratified in blood (Ex. 24:8).

All too soon, however, their awestruck reverence ebbed away. As Moses returned to the mountaintop, the people turned their adoration to the golden image of a calf (Ex. 32:1–7). Moses's intercession kept God's hand of justice from destroying the idolaters, and the Lord reaffirmed his commitment to give them the promised land (Ex. 32:11–33:1). Henceforth, however, an angel would lead them instead of God, who declared, "I will not go up among you, lest I consume you on the way, for you are a stiff-necked people" (Ex. 33:3). We might have expected the people to be relieved that God would stay at a safe distance, but they responded to "this disastrous word" with lament (Ex. 33:4). Moses himself protested, "If your presence will not go with me, do not bring us up from here. For how shall it be known that I have found favor in your sight, I and your people? Is it not in your going with us, so that we are distinct, I and your people, from every other people on the face of the earth?" (Ex. 33:15–16). To people defiled by guilt, God's presence is lethal, but his absence is unbearable.

Consequently, God provided mediators to stand between himself and his people. Moses mediated the Lord's word (Ex. 33:7–11; 34:29–35). The Lord appointed Aaron to be Israel's high priest, mediating forgiveness, cleansing, and access to God (Ex. 28–29; Lev. 8–9). And since Israel's need for cleansing was constant, God established an intergenerational succession of priestly descendants to succeed Aaron. Yet God's provision of ongoing priestly mediation through Aaron and his descendants could not be the final solution to his people's need for forgiveness, purification, and access to his presence. Grave problems beset that priesthood. Between God's designation of Aaron to be high priest (Ex. 28) and Aaron's consecration to office (Lev. 8–9), Aaron himself crafted the golden calf. Moses later recalled, "And the LORD was so angry with Aaron that he was ready to destroy him" (Deut. 9:20). After Aaron and his sons were consecrated as priests, Nadab and Abihu disregarded God's holiness and died for their disobedience (Lev. 10). In fact, the sin of every priest in Aaron's line was on display every year on the Day of Atonement, when the high priest *first* had to present a sin offering for himself (Lev. 16:1–14), *before* he sacrificed and interceded for the Israelites (16:15–34; see Heb. 5:2–3; 7:27–28; 9:7).

The author's first mention of Jesus's priestly office (Heb. 2:17–18) implies the defect of the Aaronic priesthood. God's Son "had to be made like his brothers in every respect, so that he might become a merciful and *faithful high priest* [*pistos archiereus*] in the service of God" (2:17). This statement alludes to God's word of judgment on the Aaronic priest Eli:

> Behold, the days are coming when I will cut off your strength and the strength of your father's house, so that there will not be an old man in your house.... And I will raise up for myself *a faithful priest* [LXX: *hiera piston*], who shall do according to what is in my heart and in my mind. (1 Sam. 2:31, 35)

The eradication of Eli's priestly house would begin with the violent deaths of his impious sons Hophni and Phineas (1 Sam. 4:11), and it would be completed when Solomon replaced Eli's last descendant, Abiathar, with Zadok, an Aaronic priest unrelated to Eli (1 Kings 2:26–27, 35). Yet even the Zadokite line would not fulfill the profile of a fully *faithful* priest, "who shall do according to what is in my heart and in my mind." No one belonging to the sin-stained house of Aaron could fulfill this prediction.

Hebrews 2:17–18 announces that Jesus, the Son of God, has become that faithful priest—merciful as well as faithful. He shares his people's human flesh and blood (2:14) and their experience of weakness and temptation (2:18). Consequently, he is merciful toward sinners and able to help them as they suffer temptation. But Jesus is also faithful toward God, since he endured every temptation without sin (4:15; 7:26–27). Jesus is the great high priest whose blameless integrity stands in sharp contrast to the sin that stained Aaron's priestly order.

But an objection might be raised to Jesus's priesthood. The law's requirement of genealogical descent from the tribe of Levi and the house of Aaron would disqualify Jesus, son of David and descendant of Judah, from priestly office. "For it is evident that our Lord was descended from Judah, and in connection with that tribe Moses said nothing about priests" (7:14). This problem with Christ's priesthood—his lack of Levitical-Aaronic credentials—must be addressed before his priestly ministry can be explored. So in Hebrews 4:14–7:28 our author makes his exegetical-theological case for the legitimacy of Christ's priestly qualifications, which are, in fact, superior to those of Aaron.

Priestly Qualifications

To enter God's holy presence on behalf of others according to the law, priests must fulfill two qualifications: (1) they must be identified with the people whom they represent, and (2) they must be called by God. With respect to both qualifications, the author of Hebrews builds his case for Jesus's priesthood by both comparing and contrasting Jesus and Aaron. Like Aaron, Jesus identifies with his people, sharing their human nature and their experience of weakness, temptation, and suffering. Unlike Aaron, Jesus did not succumb to temptation and commit sin (4:15; 5:2, 7–8). Like Aaron, Jesus was authorized by God's call to priestly office (5:1, 4). Unlike Aaron, Jesus received God's call not through genetic ancestry but by God's self-binding oath (5:5–6, 9–10). Let's explore these qualifications more deeply.

Identified with God's People

Even before our author introduces Jesus as the merciful high priest (2:17), he traces Christ's identification with his people to a source even deeper than human kinship. Jesus the Son of God is united with his people in two ways: (1) He and we share one Father, so we are his brothers, his children, given to him by God the Father (2:10–13). (2) He has come to share our flesh and blood, to experience our vulnerability to weakness, temptation, and suffering, and to undergo the death that daunts us (2:14–16).

We share one Father, so we are his brothers, his children. The Son's priestly qualification is rooted in a *family solidarity* that unites the eternal Son who sanctifies with the people he has come to sanctify. The Savior and the saved, the sanctifier and those sanctified, are "from one" (*ex henos*) (2:11). The Greek *henos* may be either the *masculine* genitive or the *neuter* genitive form of the cardinal number *heis*, since those forms are identical. The ESV renders this prepositional phrase as "one source" (impersonal) and the NIV says "the same family." But the mention of "many sons" in 2:10 and Christ's calling us "brothers" in 2:12 suggest that *ex henos* condenses the fuller *ex henos patros*, "[of] one Father" (NASB, CSB).[2] Through God's sovereign election, the Son shares his divine Father with those whom God gave to him (John 17:6, 9; Rom. 8:29; Eph. 1:3–6). Therefore, when he comes to their rescue through incarnation, "he is not ashamed to call them brothers" (Heb. 2:11; cf. 2:12, citing Ps. 22:22) and to call them "the children God has given me" (Heb. 2:13, citing Isa. 8:18). Even before the Son entered history to fulfill his priestly mission, God's electing grace had bound him to the human "sons" whom he would lead "to glory" through his suffering (2:10).

He has come to share our flesh and blood, our exposure to weakness, temptation, suffering, and death. Since his people "share in flesh and blood, he himself likewise partook of the same things" (2:14). The Son's incarnation made it possible for him to die on behalf of others, making "propitiation for the sins of the people" (2:17). But his incarnation also qualified the Son to continuously extend mercy and help to people beset by weakness and beleaguered by suffering: "He had to be made like his brothers in every respect, so that he might become a merciful and faithful high priest in the service of God. . . . For because he himself has suffered when tempted, he is *able to help those who are being tempted*" (2:17–18). It is Jesus's identification with his people in their weakness that prompts our author to add the adjective "merciful" (*eleēmōn*) to the expression "faithful" (derived from 1 Sam. 2:35).

2   The same elliptical Greek construction, *ex henos* ("from one"), refers to Isaac, the "one" father by whom Rebecca conceived twins (Rom. 9:10). Hebrews uses a similar construction, *aph' henos* ("from one"), to refer to Abraham the "one" father who has begotten countless descendants (Heb. 11:12).

This connection between the Son's identification with his "brothers" in temptation and his capacity to extend mercy and help is elaborated in Hebrews 4:14–5:10. Jesus and Aaron share three interrelated priestly qualifications—humanity, weakness, and empathy. First, because priest and people share a common *humanity*, the priest can represent them in God's presence. The twofold appearance of "men" (*anthrōpōn*) in the generalization of Hebrews 5:1 articulates this point: "For every high priest chosen *from among men* is appointed to act *on behalf of men* in relation to God, to offer gifts and sacrifices for sins."[3] Aaron and Christ share human nature with those for whom they intercede.

Second, both Aaron and Jesus experienced *weakness* and, in that weakness, were assaulted by temptation. As Aaron ministered to Israelites who had broken God's commandments through ignorance or waywardness, he knew that "he himself [was] beset with *weakness*" (5:2). Like Aaron and his priestly successors, our "great high priest . . . Jesus, the Son of God" can "sympathize with our *weaknesses*" because "in every respect [he] has been tempted as we are, yet without sin" (4:14–15). That final caveat—"yet without sin"—marks *the momentous difference* between Aaron's response to weakness and temptation and the response of Jesus. Aaronic priests identified not only with their brothers' weakness but also with their brothers' capitulation to temptation and sinful guilt. On the annual Day of Atonement, Aaron was "obligated to offer sacrifice for his own sins just as he does for those of the people" (5:3; see Lev. 16:6–14). Jesus, on the other hand, while entering fully into the humanity, weakness, suffering, and temptation that his people endure, withstood every attack on his faithfulness with complete and resolute obedience. He needed no sacrifice of atonement for his own sins, since he was sinless and "offered himself without blemish to God" (9:14).

---

3 Hebrews 7:5 later mentions the family ties binding the Levitical-Aaronic priests to the other Israelite tribes and clans: "And those descendants of Levi who receive the priestly office have a commandment in the law to take tithes from the people, that is, from *their brothers*."

Third, the priests' experience of weakness, temptation, and suffering enables them to extend *empathy and compassion* to fragile and failing people. Hebrews introduces Jesus's empathy with an attention-grabbing double-negative construction: "we do *not* have a high priest who *is unable to* sympathize" (4:15) means, obviously, that we *do* have a high priest who *can* sympathize with our weaknesses. Why the double negative? To highlight the thrilling surprise when we learn that, *contrary to what we might have expected*, in view of the holiness and glory of the Son of God who "has passed through the heavens" (4:14), he came near to us and became our kinsman, to share our weakness and temptation.[4]

Hebrews uses different terms to communicate the empathy expressed by Aaron and the empathy extended by Jesus. Both Aaron and Jesus share the feelings of weak sinners whom they serve. But the limit of Aaron's empathy was to "moderate one's feelings" (*metriopatheō*)[5]—that is, to control his adverse reaction to others' sins in light of his own—and so to "deal gently" (ESV) with those who violated God's law (5:2). Jesus, however, needing no atoning sacrifice for his own sin (7:27), enters *even more deeply* into his people's sorrows, "feeling along with" (*sympatheō*)[6] or deeply sympathizing with them (4:15). Jesus withstood temptation of such ferocity that Aaron would have capitulated long before the enemy's assault had reached the intensity that our sympathetic high priest endured. Christ's love for his wayward people flows from a heart so pure that his compassion—unlike the mere restraint that Aaron could muster—is unstained by even a hint of judgmentalism.

---

4   A similar grammatical construction serves the same function in 2:11: "He is not ashamed to call them brothers." In other words, *contrary to our expectations* as we consider the vast distance between his superiority to angels (1:5–13) and our finitude and fallenness, the Son is most willing ("not ashamed") to call us his brothers (and children).

5   "Μετριοπαθέω," in BAGD 515.

6   "Συμπαθέω," in L&N 25.57: "to share someone's feeling in the sense of being sympathetic with. . . . In a number of languages the closest equivalent of 'being sympathetic with' may be 'to understand completely how one feels' or 'to feel in one's heart just like someone else feels.'"

Moreover, Jesus's sympathy, grounded in his own experience of weakness, temptation, and suffering, moves beyond merely commiserating with his vulnerable people. Our high priest gives genuine *help*. Jesus's human experience of having "suffered when tempted" has given him the ability, as a "merciful" (*eleēmōn*) high priest, "to *help* [*boēthēsai*] those who are being tempted" (2:17–18). Consequently, they can "with confidence draw near to the throne of grace" and receive *mercy* [*eleos*] and *help* [*boētheian*] in time of need (4:16).

The Son's "help" to those tempted and suffering is informed by our shared *humanity*, but it is also exercised in his *divine* power. Echoes of God's promise of help to his servant Israel in Isaiah 41:8–14 are interlaced throughout the articulation in Hebrews of the Son's purpose in assuming our flesh and blood (Heb. 2:14–18):

- The Lord addresses Israel as "offspring of Abraham" (*sperma Abraam*, Isa. 41:8 LXX; cf. Heb. 2:16).
- The Lord "takes hold of" (*antilambanomai*) Abraham's offspring (Isa. 41:9 LXX) to help them (see *epilambanomai* in Heb. 2:16, rendered "helps" in ESV).[7]
- The Lord encouraged Israel, "Fear not" (*mē phobou*, Isa. 41:10, 13 LXX), and Jesus's death freed those enslaved by the fear (*phobos*) of death (Heb. 2:15).
- The Lord "helps" his servant (*boētheō*, Isa. 41:10, 13, 14 LXX; see Heb. 2:18; 4:16; 13:6).

These allusions to *God's* promises of help in Isaiah 41 are appropriate to the *eternal divine Son*. Now, having announced that this Son has come to share our flesh and blood (2:14), Hebrews links his *incarnation in weakness* to the assurance that he can extend *strong divine help* to his human family. The union of divine omnipotence and human

---

7   The replacement of *antilambanomai* in Isa. 41:9 LXX with *epilambanomai* in this allusion in Heb. 2:16 may reflect the influence of Jer. 31:32 (38:32 LXX), which is cited in Heb. 8:8–12. The Greek verbs are synonymous, and they represent the same Hebrew verb (*hazaq*) in Isa. 41:9 and Jer. 31:32.

vulnerability in the one person of Jesus Christ, the incarnate Son, makes him the ideal helper for his beleaguered people.[8]

Because our "great high priest" has "passed through the heavens" (4:14), he helps his weak and tempted people through his ceaseless intercession in the heavenly Most Holy Place (7:25–26; 10:10). But heaven is not the only venue in which he extends help. Just as his sacrifice enables us to draw near to God *in heaven* (4:15–16; 10:19–22), so also our divine helper draws near to us *on earth*. In times past, God promised ancient believers, "I will not leave you or forsake you" (Josh 1:5; cf. Gen. 28:15; Deut. 31:6, 8; 1 Sam. 12:22; 1 Kings 6:13; 8:57; 1 Chron. 28:20; Neh. 9:17, 19, 31; Pss. 37:28; 94:14; Isa. 41:17; 42:16). This promise still stands under the new covenant, as our author assures his audience:

> Be content with what you have, for he has said, "I will never leave you nor forsake you." So we can confidently say,

> "The Lord is my helper [*boēthos*];
>   I will not fear;
> what can man do to me?" (Heb. 13:5–6).

This affirmation of trust in the Lord, our helper, is followed by the declaration that he remains ever constant and ever present: "Jesus Christ is the same yesterday and today and forever" (13:8). This Christological statement links the incarnate Son's *human* name ("Jesus") and his *messianic* title ("Christ") with the *divine* immutability ("the same") for which he is praised as "Lord" in Psalm 102:25–27 (Heb. 1:10–12). This brief confession (eleven words in Greek) encapsulates the Christology of Hebrews and of the church's historic creeds: humanity and

8 As the Definition of Chalcedon expressed the mystery revealed in the New Testament, Christ's divine nature and human nature each *retain their distinctive attributes* without diminishing *the genuine unity* of the person of the God-man. See "The Chalcedonian Definition: Agreed at the Fourth Ecumenical Council at Chalcedon in 451," Early Church Texts, accessed June 5, 2023, https://earlychurchtexts.com/main/chalcedon/chalcedonian_definition.shtml.

deity united in one person for the redemptive mission that could be accomplished in no other way.

How does our great high priest, who intercedes on our behalf *in heaven*, make good his promise never to leave or forsake us as we trek through *this world's* wilderness? The eternal Holy Spirit through whom Jesus offered himself on our behalf (9:15) is now bearing witness to us through ancient Scripture (10:15), through apostolic testimony (2:3–4), and through the instruction and example of faithful shepherds (13:7).

Called by God

Access into the presence of the living God, the high and holy sovereign of all, was by invitation only. "No one takes this honor for himself, but only when called by God, as Aaron was" (Heb. 5:4). Even for merely human royal courts in the ancient Near East, the king alone decided who would be admitted to his throne room (2 Sam. 14:21–28; Est. 4:11). How much more, then, the Lord of all creation, whose holiness is so intense that it poses lethal danger to sin-defiled creatures (Ex. 33:20; see Gen. 32:30; Isa. 6:5)!

In the wilderness, God demonstrated in three ways that he alone retains the right to call priests to enter his presence to intercede for others. First, God specifically told Moses that his brother Aaron was to be Israel's first high priest: "Then bring near to you Aaron your brother, and his sons with him, from among the people of Israel, to serve me as priests" (Ex. 28:1). Second, the Lord commanded a restrictive regulation controlling entrance into the tent's inner chamber, the Most Holy Place (Ex. 26:31–34; Lev. 16:2–4, 11–16). Only the high priest could pass through the inner veil to sprinkle blood on the atonement cover of the ark of the covenant (Heb. 9:6–7). "No one may be in the tent of meeting from the time he enters to make atonement in the Holy Place until he comes out" (Lev. 16:17). Third, the destruction that God wreaked on Korah, Dathan, and Abiram for their presumptuous demand to seize priestly privilege showed that God called only Aaron and his sons to minister in his sanctuary (Num. 16). In the sequel to the rebels' destruction, the Lord caused Aaron's rod alone (among rods representing all Israel's tribes) to blossom miraculously (Num. 17; see Heb. 9:4). So God asserted in no uncertain terms that he had called Aaron alone to serve as Israel's high priestly mediator.[9]

This background highlights the difficulty that our author raised concerning Jesus's descent from the tribe of Judah, which placed him outside both the tribe of Levi and the specific lineage of Aaron (Heb. 7:14). Psalm 110 answers this dilemma. By alluding to and then citing (Heb. 1:3, 13) the psalm's first verse,

> The LORD says to my Lord,
>   "Sit at my right hand,
> until I make your enemies your footstool" (Ps. 110:1),

our author has echoed Jesus himself, who applied this *royal* enthronement edict to the Messiah (Mark 12:35–37; 14:62). Other New Testament authors likewise affirmed the psalm's fulfillment in Christ's resurrection, ascension, and heavenly enthronement (Acts 2:34; Rom. 8:34; 1 Cor. 15:25; Eph. 1:20). Yet *only Hebrews* cites and explores the *priestly* appointment edict in Psalm 110:4:

> The LORD has sworn
>   and will not change his mind,
> "You are a priest forever
>   after the order of Melchizedek."

Our author unfolds the significance of Psalm 110:4 for the issue of Jesus's priestly qualification in four steps: (1) This verse demonstrates that Jesus, like Aaron, did not seize the priestly office for himself but was called to it by God (Heb. 5:5–10). (2) The historical account of Abraham's meeting with Melchizedek (Gen. 14:17–20) demonstrates (a) the merger of kingship and priesthood in the order of Melchize-

---

9   Another confirmation of the Lord's call to Aaron was the appearance of the Lord's glory at Aaron's ordination and the Lord's sending fire out to consume Aaron's ordination sacrifice (Lev. 9:22–24), although Hebrews does not mention this incident.

dek, (b) the absence of issues related to genealogy (parentage, birth, death) for the priestly order of Melchizedek, and (c) the superiority of Melchizedek's priesthood to that of Levi (Heb. 7:1–10). (3) The genealogical principle that is essential to Aaron's priestly order is transcended by the qualification of "indestructible life," which constitutes Jesus "a priest *forever*, after the order of Melchizedek" (7:16–17; see 7:15–19, 23–25, 28). (4) The psalm further affirms that Jesus's priesthood, unlike that of Aaron and his descendants, is eternally secured by God's inviolable oath:

> The Lord *has sworn*
>   and *will not change his mind*. (7:21; see 7:20–22, 28)

We will consider each of these four steps in turn.

The first step in unfolding the significance of Psalm 110:4 draws a straightforward parallel between Aaron and Christ. Both fulfilled the essential requirement of *divine appointment* rather than self-promotion: "No one takes this honor [of priestly office] for himself, but only when called by God, *just as Aaron* was. *So also Christ* did not exalt himself to be made high priest but was appointed by [God]" (Heb. 5:4–5). In support of this point, the author cites Psalm 2:7, the first Old Testament quotation in the catena of Hebrews 1,[10] and places Psalm 110:4 alongside it. The parallel structure of these two words of divine address—"you are my Son" and "you are a priest forever"—highlights God's recognition, approval, and sovereign appointment of "the Son of God" to be the "great high priest who has passed through the heavens" (Heb. 4:14).

The second step considers the historical record of Abraham's meeting with Melchizedek in Genesis 14. After a sobering exhortation to persevering faith (Heb. 5:11–6:13), the author returns to the priestly order of Melchizedek by way of a summons to imitate believing Abraham,

---

10 It is no coincidence that the catena of Old Testament quotations that *opens* with Ps. 2:7 (Heb. 1:5) *closes* with Ps. 110:1 (Heb. 1:13) and that both are alluded to in the sermon's prologue: "his Son . . . sat down at the right hand" (Heb. 1:2–3).

who met the original Melchizedek (6:14–20). When Melchizedek's priestly order again takes center stage, our author places Psalm 110:4 into the context of the meeting between Abraham and that ancient priest-king (see Gen. 14:17–20). The author's close reading of Genesis 14 draws from that text insights that illumine the connection between Psalm 110:1 and 110:4. Three points stand out in this second step (Heb. 7:1–10): (1) Since ancient Melchizedek (which means, "king of righteousness," 7:2) was both *king* of Salem (which means "king of peace," 7:2) and *priest* of the Most High God, his "order" transcends the division of roles and authority between kings and priests in Israel. The individual whom the Lord addressed in Psalm 110 would be both *a king* enthroned at God's right hand, executing justice and victory over enemies, and *a priest* authorized to enter God's sanctuary. (2) Since the Spirit led Moses to omit mention of Melchizedek's genealogy, birth, and death, Genesis presents him as a template for a priestly order for which genealogical descent is *not* a requirement for divine appointment. (3) The interactions between Abraham and Melchizedek—Abraham giving Melchizedek a tithe of battle spoils and Melchizedek blessing Abraham in God's name—signal that the patriarch rightly recognized the *mediatorial superiority* of Melchizedek. Moreover, in these mutual transactions Abraham acted as a representative of his descendant Levi (and of Levi's descendant Aaron). In effect, therefore, Levi and Aaron (through Abraham) acknowledged that Melchizedek's mediatorial ministry was superior to their own (Heb. 7:9–10). Against the backdrop of Genesis 14, Psalm 110:4 introduces Melchizedek's "successor," who fulfills the pattern set by that ancient figure: a king who is a priest, whose divine appointment is not mediated by genealogy, and whose ministry is superior to that of Aaron.

The third step in the exploration of Psalm 110:4 draws out the implications of the phrase "priest *forever*" (7:17; see 7:15–19, 23–25, 28). Levitical-Aaronic priestly qualification through genealogy was intertwined with the death of each generation of priests. But Psalm 110:4 speaks of a priestly order that transcends both death and genealogy, for here the Lord installs a priest who ministers *forever*. His qualification is not derived from "a legal requirement concerning bodily descent" (or "the law of a fleshly commandment," Greek *nomon entolēs sarkinēs*) but rests on "the power of an indestructible life" (7:16). He needs no successor but "holds his priesthood permanently, because he continues forever" (7:24). Thus, "he always lives to make intercession" for those who trust him and, therefore, can save them completely and eternally (7:25).[11]

The fourth and final step in the author's unfolding of the significance of Psalm 110:4 for Jesus's better priesthood is *God's irrevocable oath,* which complements the priest's endless life to secure the permanence of his tenure:

And it was not without an oath. For those who formerly became priests were made such without an oath, but this one was made a priest with an oath by the one who said to him:

"The Lord has sworn
    and will not change his mind,
'You are a priest forever.'" (Heb. 7:20–21)

By swearing an oath, the Lord summoned himself to be the witness *and the enforcer* of his solemn promise. If God were to break his promise and violate his covenant, he would inflict on himself the covenant curse of utter destruction, symbolized by blood and the carcasses of animals slain in covenant-ratification rituals (Gen. 15:9–20; Jer. 34:18–20). Of course, God's death is as impossible as his faithless breach of covenant.

So Hebrews demonstrates that Psalm 110, read against the backdrop of Genesis 14, establishes not only the *legitimacy* of Jesus's qualification for priesthood but also its *superiority* to the priesthood of Aaron.

---

11 In 7:25, the Greek prepositional phrase *eis to panteles* (ESV: "to the uttermost") can refer either to perpetuity/eternity or to completeness (note the negative construction in Luke 13:11: "could not fully straighten herself"). "Παντελής," in BAGD 608. Since Christ's power to save his people results from his endless life and his ceaseless intercession, the temporal sense seems dominant here: "forever."

Fulfilling the pattern of the ancient Melchizedek, Jesus is the priest-king who mediates God's blessing to Abraham and his offspring, whose indestructible life renders irrelevant the issue of genealogy, and whose priestly tenure is eternally secured by God's divine oath.

Priestly Consecration: "Perfection"

Formal recognition of a priest's authorization to approach God on others' behalf entails a rite of consecration or ordination. For Aaron and his sons, this ritual involved washing, clothing, anointing, sacrificing a bull and ram, applying the animals' blood to the priests' bodies, further sprinkling with blood, and eating a ceremonial meal (Lev. 8). The Hebrew verbal construction describing this consecration/ordination rite is *mille' yad*—literally, "fill (one's) hand." In the Septuagint, it is translated *teleioō tas cheiras* (or simply *teleioō*) (Ex. 29:9, 29, 33, 35; Lev. 8:33; 16:32; 21:10; Num. 3:3 LXX). In other texts the Hebrew noun *mellu'im,* derived from the same verb, designates priestly consecration, and this term is translated *teleiōsis* in the Septuagint (Ex. 29:22, 26, 27, 31, 34; Lev. 8:22, 28–33 LXX).

This Old Testament linguistic background unlocks the author's use of the verb "perfect" (*teleioō*) and the noun "perfection" (*teleiōsis*). Elsewhere in the New Testament, as in ancient Greek literature generally, this word group expresses completion or perfection (that is, "lacking in nothing," James 1:4).[12] In some passages in Hebrews, we see this general sense of the *teleio-* cognate group, which the English "perfect/perfection" represents well (Heb. 6:1 [ESV: "maturity"]; 11:40; 12:23). But the Septuagint's specialized use of *teleioō* and *teleiōsis* to refer to priestly ordination is also in play in such passages as these:

> For it was fitting that he, for whom and by whom all things exist, in bringing many sons to glory, should *make* the founder of their salvation *perfect* [*teleiōsai*, aorist active infinitive] through suffering. (Heb. 2:10)

12 "τέλειος" and "τελειόω," in BAGD 809–10.

And *having been made perfect* [*teleiothēs*, aorist passive participle], [Jesus] became the source of eternal salvation to all who obey him, *having been designated* [*prosagoreuthēs*, aorist passive participle] by God a high priest after the order of Melchizedek. (Heb. 5:9–10, my translation)

For the law appoints men in their weakness as high priests, but the word of the oath, which came later than the law, appoints a Son who *has been made perfect* [*teteleiōmenon*, perfect passive participle] forever. (Heb. 7:28)

Regarding such statements, Geerhardus Vos writes, "As to the term *perfection* (*teleioosis*) [sic], we must adhere strictly to the meaning *fitting for the office*."[13] Similarly, Moisés Silva comments that in Hebrews the verb *teleioō* "is used nine times, nearly always with OT cultic overtones. As such it means 'to make perfect' in the sense of (priestly) consecration."[14]

Although the use of "perfection" (*teleioō, teleiōsis*) in Hebrews is strongly indebted to the Septuagint's usage to refer to priestly ordination, Hebrews enriches the concept of perfection as consecration in a couple of ways. First, drawing on the sense of perfection as flawless completion, Hebrews stresses that Jesus's *blameless obedience*, to the point of death, is the consecrating event that marks his induction into superior priestly office. It is *because* "he learned obedience through what he suffered" (5:8) that Jesus can be the sympathetic high priest, even as he remained sinless, holy, innocent, and unstained, throughout the temptations and sufferings of his earthly life (4:15; 7:26). Aaron and his sons were "perfected"—that is, consecrated—through rituals by which water, blood, and oil were applied to their *flesh*. But such rites could not "perfect" the *conscience* of priests or other worshipers (9:9). Christ, on the other hand, was consecrated to priestly office through his flawless and comprehensive obedience, climaxing in his death on the

---

13 Geerhardus Vos, *The Teaching of the Epistle to the Hebrews* (Grand Rapids, MI: Eerdmans, 1956), 104.

14 "τέλος," in *NIDNTTE* 4:447.

cross, fulfilling God's will (10:10). Graham Hughes observes, "Jesus's priestly qualifications are dependent on, or emergent from, his obedient relationship with God."[15] We could say that Jesus's obedience in "offering his body" in death "filled his hand" (to recall the Hebrew idiom) with *his own* sacrificial blood to carry into the heavenly sanctuary for our forgiveness (9:12).

This observation—that Jesus's consecration to priestly office ("perfection") was contingent on his obedience through suffering, climaxing in the offering of his body in death (10:10)—might initially appear to support the conclusion drawn by David Moffitt in his influential monograph, *Atonement and the Logic of the Resurrection in the Epistle to the Hebrews*, that Jesus's priestly ministry did not begin until he rose from the dead and ascended to heaven.[16] Moffitt observes that Hebrews 8:4 "seems to say that Jesus was *not* a priest on earth. In fact, 8:4 clearly locates Jesus's priestly ministry in heaven, after his life and death on earth."[17] R. B. Jamieson summarizes the position of Moffitt and others: "Strictly speaking, Jesus offers himself in the heavenly sanctuary after his resurrection, not on the cross."[18] Since Moffitt understands 8:4 as excluding priestly activity by Jesus on earth, prior to his resurrection, Moffitt argues "that Jesus's death on the cross is not the place or the primary means of atonement for the author of Hebrews. . . . The great atoning moment of the incarnation occurred not when Jesus was crucified but after he was resurrected and ascended into heaven."[19]

15 Graham Hughes, *Hebrews and Hermeneutics: The Epistle to the Hebrews as a New Testament Example of Biblical Interpretation* (Cambridge: Cambridge University Press, 1979), 33.

16 David M. Moffitt, *Atonement and the Logic of the Resurrection in the Epistle to the Hebrews*, NovTSup 141 (Leiden: Brill, 2011). He has subsequently presented his view in essays that appear in David M. Moffitt, *Rethinking the Atonement: New Perspectives on Jesus's Death, Resurrection, and Ascension* (Grand Rapids, MI: Baker Academic, 2022).

17 Moffitt, *Atonement and the Logic of the Resurrection*, 198 (emphasis in original).

18 R. B. Jamieson, "When and Where Did Jesus Offer Himself? A Taxonomy of Recent Scholarship on Hebrews," *CBR* 15, no. 3 (2017): 352.

19 David M. Moffitt, "Blood, Life, and Atonement: Reassessing Hebrews' Christological Appropriation of Yom Kippur," in *Rethinking the Atonement*, 87–88.

Moffitt appropriately corrects previous scholarly neglect of the centrality of Christ's bodily resurrection and ascension for the theology of Christ's redemptive achievement articulated in Hebrews. The author's use of the Mosaic Yom Kippur ritual as a template to demonstrate the superiority of Christ's priesthood and his sacrifice does present Jesus's death, resurrection, and ascension *as a unified complex* that achieves, for "those who draw near to God through him" (7:25), what animal victims' blood could not: once-for-all forgiveness of sins, cleansing of conscience, and access to God's presence.

On the other hand, Moffitt's corrective (in favor of the resurrection and ascension) becomes a one-sided overcorrection when he denies that Jesus's priesthood included his earthly ministry and when he therefore reduces Jesus's death to "*the* paradigm of righteous suffering" and "Jesus' *preparation* for his high-priestly ministry and atoning offering," which occur only in heaven and only after his exaltation.[20] The author's comment, "if [Jesus] were on earth, he would not be a priest at all" (8:4), is an implication of the previous argument that Christ's priesthood according to the order of Melchizedek surpasses the ministry of those qualified by a law of genealogy to serve in a merely earthly sanctuary. That statement is not intended to deny that Jesus, *in his death on earth*, acted as the great high priest who offered his body and blood as the once-for-all sacrifice that propitiates God's wrath against the guilty, cleanses their defiled consciences, and delivers them from the fear of death (2:14–18). Jesus's death "redeems them from the transgressions committed under the first covenant" (9:15). On the Day of Atonement, the *slaughter* of the sacrificial bull and goat, no less than the *presentation of their blood* in the Most Holy Place, was exclusively the privilege and task of *the high priest* (Lev. 16:11–15).[21] To argue that Jesus's death on earth was a non-atoning

---

20 Moffitt, *Atonement and the Logic of the Resurrection*, 285 (emphasis in original).

21 Moffitt, "Blood, Life, and Atonement," 95, argues that on Yom Kippur "the death or slaughter of the victim, while necessary to procure the blood, has no particular atoning significance in and of itself." In his view, the death of the victim is soteriologically

event, performed by *one who was not (yet) consecrated as a priest*, is to put asunder priestly actions that both the Yom Kippur rite and the theology of Hebrews hold together.[22]

Luke-Acts profiles two phases of Jesus's royal messianic office in ministry, first in suffering and subsequently in glory (Luke 24:26). First, at his baptism Jesus was anointed by God's Spirit and addressed by God as messianic Son and King, in words alluding to Psalm 2:6–7 (Luke 3:21–22; see 4:17–21; Acts 10:38). Then, at his resurrection-ascension Jesus was enthroned in glory at God's right hand in fulfillment of Psalm 110:1 (Acts 2:33–36). So, also, Hebrews profiles two phases of Jesus's priestly office and ministry, first in obedience through suffering climaxing in sacrificial death and, subsequently, in entrance into God's heavenly sanctuary to intercede without ceasing for his people. First, he "came into the world" (Heb. 10:5), partaking of flesh and blood (2:14) and receiving the body prepared for him in order to do God's will through obedient suffering, achieving the result that "we have been sanctified through the offering of the body of Jesus Christ once for all" (10:10). The earthly locus of this first phase of Christ's priestly ministry—the shedding of his own blood in death as a vicarious sacrifice—is reinforced by the allusion to Isaiah 53:12 in Hebrews 9:28: "Christ, having been offered *once to bear the sins of many*, will appear a second time, not to deal with sin but to save those who are eagerly waiting for him." Then, at his resurrection-ascension Jesus "passed through the heavens" (4:14) and "entered once for all into the holy places" (9:12), "into heaven itself, now to appear in the presence of God on our behalf" (9:24). As the Westminster Shorter Catechism

---

insignificant because the Day of Atonement involved no symbolism of substitution, in which animals without blemish endured covenant curse (death) in place of spiritually defiled humans. Others challenge Moffitt's denial of substitution symbolism in the Mosaic law. See, e.g., R. B. Jamieson, *Jesus' Death and Heavenly Offering in Hebrews*, SNTSMS 172 (Cambridge: Cambridge University Press, 2019), 135–41, 183–87, cited in Brandon D. Crowe, "Son and Priest, Then and Now: Christology and Redemptive History in Hebrews in Light of the History of Interpretation," *WTJ* 84 (2022): 32.

22 For further discussion of evidence in Hebrews for Jesus's priestly office and ministry both in his earthly obedience and suffering and in his heavenly exaltation, see Crowe, "Son and Priest," 19–38.

rightly affirms, "Christ, as our Redeemer, executeth the offices of a prophet, of a *priest*, and of a king, *both in his estate of humiliation and exaltation.*"[23]

The second way in which Hebrews enriches the perfection theme concerns the conscience-cleansing effects of Jesus's sacrifice for *believers*, who through him now participate in the priestly privilege of approaching God's holy throne of grace. The gifts and sacrifices offered by Aaronic priests could not "perfect [*teleioō*] the conscience of the worshiper" but accomplished only external cleansing (9:9; see 7:11, 19). That is why access to the ancient sanctuary was so severely restricted: only priests could enter the first chamber, and only the high priest could go into the Most Holy Place (9:6–8). But Christ's blood purifies our conscience "to serve the living God" (9:14). In fact, "by a single offering he has perfected [*teteleiōken*, perfect active indicative] for all time those who are being sanctified [*hagiazomenous*, present passive participle]" (10:14). Here the contrast in verb tenses is significant: believers' personal sanctification remains an ongoing, incomplete, and lifelong process, but through his sacrifice Christ "has perfected" them once-for-all and forever. As a result, believers have "confidence to enter the holy places by the blood of Jesus . . . with our hearts sprinkled clean from an evil conscience" (10:19, 22). F. F. Bruce comments, "There is much in this epistle about the attainment of perfection in the sense of *unimpeded access to God and unbroken communion with him*, but in this as in other things it is Christ who leads the way."[24] Whereas the law spoke of forgiveness of ordinary Israelites' sins and cleansing from ritual defilement, the language of "perfecting"—ordination to, in Bruce's words, "unimpeded access to God"—was reserved for the priesthood. Now, however, all who draw near to God through Jesus's priestly mediation have been "perfected" and can approach God, offering worship that pleases him (12:28; 13:15–16).

---

23 Westminster Shorter Catechism, question 23 (emphasis added).

24 F. F. Bruce, *The Epistle to the Hebrews*, NICNT, rev. ed. (Grands Rapids, MI: Eerdmans, 1990), 80 (emphasis added).

Conclusion

We need a priestly mediator who can identify with us in our weakness and temptation but who also is qualified to approach the holy God on our behalf. The Levitical-Aaronic priesthood instituted in the law of Moses was God's gracious but imperfect provision for our need, since each member of that priestly order both sinned and died, only to be followed by another generation of flawed intercessors.

Hebrews demonstrates that our need for a perfect priest—merciful and faithful, installed by God's oath, living forever, interceding without ceasing, and saving to the uttermost—is met only in Jesus, the Son of God. Jesus's endless life and ministry were foreshadowed in the account of Abraham's encounter with Melchizedek (Gen. 14:17–20) and foretold in Psalm 110. Those Scriptures testify not only that Jesus satisfies the criteria of identification with humans and authorization by God but also that Jesus's priestly qualifications far surpass those of Aaron and his descendants. Jesus has been perfected—consecrated to enter God's heavenly sanctuary on our behalf—not through external rites but through his own blameless fulfillment of God's will, both in active obedience and in sacrificial death. Assured that Jesus is the great high priest we need, we eagerly anticipate the author's exploration of his mediatorial ministry (8:2–10:25), to which we now turn.

6

Jesus's Once-for-All, Conscience-Perfecting Sacrifice

The blood of the eternal covenant.

HEBREWS 13:20

Blood and Friendship with God

Israel's priests fulfilled many roles, but those most relevant to the presentation in Hebrews of Jesus's priestly ministry are sacrifice, intercession, and providing access to the presence of God.[1] These three themes are interrelated. The shed blood of sacrificial victims was the basis for the priests' petitions, in word and in action, for God to forgive his people's sins. The Lord's forgiveness, granted in response to sacrifice and intercession, would issue in covenant communion between himself and his sinful but beloved worshipers.

Blood was a pervasive component of Israel's worship on a daily, weekly, monthly, and yearly basis (Num. 28–29). Every day, morning

---

[1] In addition to these responsibilities, priests were custodians and teachers of the law, the covenant treaty binding the Lord and his people (Deut. 31:9–13; 33:10; Ezra 7:1–10; Jer. 2:8; Mal. 2:4–7). They also consulted with tribal elders and judges in legal decisions (Deut. 17:8–10). Israel's tithes were brought to the Lord's sanctuary, in part to provide for Levites, widows, and orphans (Deut. 14:28–29). So, possibly, priests and their Levitical assistants administered this financial relief for those who were destitute and dependent. See P. Ellingworth, "Priests," in *NDBT* 696–701.

and evening, lambs were sacrificed. More lambs were offered each Sabbath. Each new month, two bulls, a ram, and seven lambs were slain. The shedding of blood was integral to the annual feasts: Passover, Weeks, Trumpets, the Day of Atonement, and Booths. Blood flowed for burnt offerings, peace offerings, sin offerings, and guilt offerings (Lev. 1–6). At the inauguration of the Mosaic covenant, blood was thrown on God's altar and the people (Ex. 24:1–11). At the consecration of the Aaronic priests, blood was thrown on the altar, poured out at its base, applied to the priests (earlobes, thumbs, and toes), and sprinkled on their vestments (29:15–28).

Why so much blood? Why so much death? The priests' central mission was to mediate between the Lord and his sinful people, who can experience life only in intimate communion with him. Why, then, is the pathway into the presence of God—whom to know is eternal life (John 17:3)—soaked in blood and strewn with corpses? The answer lies in the dilemma (considered in chap. 5) that God alone could resolve: human sin makes divine immanence no longer life-giving but, rather, lethal. Because sin is high treason against the infinitely worthy Creator, its just punishment is nothing less than death (Gen. 2:16–17; Rom. 3:23; 5:12; 7:5–13). Adam and Eve sensed this just sentence, so they hid among the trees of the garden. Israel too feared death if the Lord were to address them directly (Ex. 20:18–21).

Only one alternative could avert the destruction of traitors against God's covenant: the covenant Lord himself must supply a blameless substitute to endure the cursed death in the rebels' stead. This principle of substitutionary suffering emerges in patriarchal history at the Lord's provision of a ram to die instead of Abraham's son Isaac: "God will provide for himself the lamb for a burnt offering" (Gen. 22:8). It was enacted in the Mosaic rituals in which worshipers laid hands on the heads of animals about to be slain, designating those beasts as proxies to die in place of guilty humans (Lev. 4:4, 15, 24, 29, 32; see 16:21–22). The law's system of substitutionary sacrifice, in which flawless (animal) victims endured the death due to the guilty, painted the backdrop for Isaiah's portrait of the suffering servant:

But he was pierced for our transgressions;
   he was crushed for our iniquities;
. . . .
All we like sheep have gone astray;
   we have turned—every one—to his own way;
and the Lord has laid on him
   the iniquity of us all.
. . . .
when his soul makes an offering for guilt,
   he shall see his offspring; he shall prolong his days.
. . . .
by his knowledge shall the righteous one, my servant,
   make many to be accounted righteous,
   and he shall bear their iniquities. (Isa. 53:5–6, 10–11)

Hebrews, in concert with the ancient Scriptures, asserts that the champion who won our salvation walked a bloodstained pathway to lead "many sons to glory" (Heb. 2:10). Our great high priest enables us to enter the heavenly Most Holy Place by his own blood (10:19–20). His once-for-all sacrifice is the basis for his ceaseless intercession, securing for his people access to the life-giving presence of God (4:16; 7:25; 10:22).

Sacrifice

According to the law, animal sacrifices conveyed various expressions of worship toward God.[2] Whole burnt offerings symbolized the consecration of the worshipers to the service of the Lord (Lev. 1; 6:9–13). Firstfruits and firstborn offerings acknowledged that families, crops, herds, and flocks were God's gracious gifts and remained his property to be managed by his human stewards (Ex. 13:11–17; Lev. 2:14–16; Deut. 15:19–20). Thanksgiving offerings expressed gratitude for the Lord's generous kindness (Lev. 7:12; Ps. 107:22). Fellowship or

---

2 See R. T. Beckwith, "Sacrifice," in *NDBT* 754–62.

peace sacrifices, which were consumed in part by the worshipers and their families, represented the restoration of covenant communion between Lord and servant (Lev. 3; 7:11–36). The Passover seder, eaten by whole families, celebrated Israel's redemption from slavery at the exodus (Ex. 12; Num. 28:16–25; Deut. 16:1–8). Sin and guilt offerings, the Day of Atonement, and rites of cleansing symbolized the removal of spiritual defilement and liability to God's righteous wrath (Lev. 4–7; 12, 14–16). Hebrews focuses on this last category of sacrifices as foreshadowing Christ's death to atone for sin and cleanse the conscience.

Hebrews elaborates Christ's self-sacrifice from a variety of perspectives, each of which enriches our grasp of the redemptive power of his death on our behalf. Jesus died to *deliver* his family from slavery to the fear of death (Heb. 2:14–16). His death *propitiated* God's wrath against them (2:17–18). By his blood, he secured the *atonement* for sins—*purification* of conscience—that the high priest's actions on the Day of Atonement, repeated annually, could not achieve (9:6–14, 24–28; 10:5–10). Christ's death accomplished *redemption* from the transgressions committed under the old covenant, thereby *inaugurating a new covenant* and guaranteeing its promise of complete forgiveness (9:15–20; 10:12–18). His blood constitutes the better sacrifices that *consecrate* his people as the *heavenly things* that belong to God's heavenly sanctuary (9:21–24).

Deliverance and Propitiation

Although Hebrews primarily expounds the significance of Jesus's death in the categories of Israel's *priesthood*, his suffering is portrayed also in *royal* imagery. As King, Christ rescues God's people, defeating their enemy, the devil, through his death. Jesus has been "*crowned* with glory and honor because of the suffering of death," since "by the grace of God" he "taste[d] death for everyone" (Heb. 2:9). He is the *archēgos* of salvation, whose suffering led God's many sons to glory (2:10). The title *archēgos*, variously translated "founder" (ESV), "captain" (KJV), "pioneer" (CSB, NIV), "source"

(HCSB), or "originator" (NASB) appears four times in the New Testament, always applied to Jesus as one who leads others into life, salvation, and faith (see Acts 3:15; 5:31; Heb. 12:2).[3] In Hebrews 2:10, in view of the military imagery soon to follow, "captain" or "champion" (proposed by William Lane) seems to fit the author's intention.[4]

This redemptive mission required the Son to partake in human flesh and blood (2:14). Such embodied life cemented the divine Son's solidarity with his human siblings, and it made it possible for him, whose "years will have no end" (1:12), to undergo death, the terrifying threat that had kept them "subject to lifelong slavery" (2:14–15). Here the imagery is explicitly *military* and, therefore, *royal*. Israel's kings were charged to take the lead in defending God's people and combatting their enemies (1 Sam. 8:20). Saul initially became the royal warrior (1 Sam. 10). When he failed, David, newly anointed, waged war in the name of the Lord (1 Sam. 17). This royal-military calling is expressed in our author's beloved Psalm 110, in which the Lord promises to subdue Messiah's enemies under his feet (Heb. 1:13; 10:12–13). In his flesh and by his death the Son came to "destroy" (ESV) or "nullify" (*katargeō*)[5] the devil, "who has the power of death" (Heb. 2:14). The devil has the power of death because he lured humanity's original parents into sin and, thus, into death (Gen. 2:16–17; 3:1–19; John 8:44; Rom. 5:12–19; 1 Cor. 15:21–22). But even as the sentence of death began to infect fallen humankind, God announced the coming of an offspring of the woman who would combat and conquer the enemy (Gen. 3:15). The result of Christ's destruction of the death-dealing devil is the *liberation* of that tyrant's slaves. The Greek verb rendered "deliver" (*apallassō*) in Hebrews 2:15 elsewhere represents release from legal liability (Luke 12:58), diseases (Acts 19:12),

3 In its thirty-five appearances in the LXX, *archēgos* typically refers to the leaders of families or clans (e.g., Ex. 6:14; Num. 10:4). It refers to military leaders in Judg. 5:2; 9:44; 11:6, 11; 2 Chron. 23:14.
4 William L. Lane, *Hebrews 1–8*, WBC 47A (Dallas: Word, 1991), 56–57.
5 The semantic range of *katargeō* includes "render ineffective" (e.g., Gal. 3:17; Eph. 2:15) as well as "abolish, wipe out" (e.g., Rom. 6:6; 2 Thess. 2:8; 2 Tim. 1:10).

marital vows,[6] debt, and legal condemnation.[7] Since those whom the Son "delivers" have been "subject to lifelong slavery" (Heb. 2:15), their rescue is liberation from oppression. By his death, the champion of the family of God nullified the devil's power to enslave the offspring of Abraham by the fear of death (2:15–16).[8]

Having employed this royal-military imagery to describe Christ's death and its effect, our author turns to *priestly* concepts to explain the reason that Christ's death frees the devil's slaves: "he had to be made like his brothers in every respect, so that he might become a merciful and faithful *high priest . . . to make propitiation* for the sins of the people" (2:17). The blending of the motifs of royal combat and priestly propitiation flows from Psalm 110, in which God addresses the exalted king (Ps. 110:1) as "priest forever after the order of Melchizedek" (Ps. 110:4). The verb "make propitiation" (*hilaskomai*) expresses the deflection of God's wrath from sinners who deserve destruction at God's righteous hands. It is implied that the wrath has been redirected to their substitute in his death.[9]

The cognate noun *hilastērion*, which in Hebrews 9:5 refers to the "mercy seat" (or "atonement cover") on the ark of the covenant, is used by Paul in Romans to refer to the wrath-averting effect of Christ's death: "For all have sinned and fall short of the glory of God, and are justified by his grace as a gift, through the redemption that is in Christ Jesus, whom God put forward as a *propitiation* by his blood, to

---

6   "Ἀπαλλάσσω," in James Hope Moulton and George Milligan, *The Vocabulary of the Greek Testament Illustrated from the Papyri and Other Non-Literary Sources* (London: Hodder and Stoughton, 1930; repr. Grand Rapids, MI: Eerdmans, 1976), 52.

7   "Ἀπαλλάσσω," in Henry George Liddell and Robert Scott, *Greek-English Lexicon*, 8th ed. (New York: American Book Company, 1897), 160–61. See also entries on "ἀπαλλάσσω" in BAGD 80 ("free, release"); L&N 37.127 ("set free").

8   Lane, *Hebrews 1–8*, 61–63, argues that the conceptual background for the portrayal of Christ's triumph over the devil and liberation of his captives is to be seen in the prophets' characterization of the Lord as divine warrior (e.g., Isa. 42:13; 49:24–26; 59:15–20), which is picked up by Jesus to explain why he, having bound the strong man (Satan), can set Satan's slaves free by exorcising demons (Luke 11:21–22).

9   Leon Morris, *The Apostolic Preaching of the Cross* (Grand Rapids, MI: Eerdmans, 1955), 174–80; see 123–85 on propitiation throughout the Bible. See also "ἱλάσκομαι," in *NIDNTTE* 2:531–41.

be received by faith" (Rom. 3:23–25). Paul had announced that "the wrath of God is revealed from heaven against all ungodliness and un- righteousness of men" (Rom. 1:18). This personal anger of God, the just Judge, is toward pagan idolaters but also toward Jews who have his written law but violate it (Rom. 1:18–3:20). Thus, the "all" in "all have sinned" is all-inclusive, embracing Gentiles and Jews alike. But Jesus Christ's shed blood turned away this divine wrath from "all who believe" (Rom. 3:22), who consequently "have peace with God through our Lord Jesus Christ" (Rom. 5:1).

The author to the Hebrews is vividly aware that "it is a fearful thing to fall into the hands of the living God" (Heb. 10:31). For this reason his announcement that Jesus, as our merciful and faithful high priest, has offered himself in death "to make propitiation for the sins of the people" (2:17) resounds as hope-engendering good news.

Atonement, Forgiveness, and Cleansing

"Propitiation" expresses an essential dimension of what Christ ac- complished by his tasting death on others' behalf (2:9), but it focuses on what Jesus's death *eliminated*: God's wrath, which we deserve, is no longer directed toward us. Hebrews, however, gives more attention to what believers *gain* as a result of Christ's sacrifice. By his blood, our *consciences are cleansed* from sin's defilement; and we are thus rendered *pure, acceptable* to enter God's holy presence. Jesus's sacrificial death not only rescues his people from the devil's domination, from enslavement to the fear of death, and from God's wrath but also brings forgiveness and the cleansing of consciences that qualifies them to draw near to God's throne of grace.

Once-for-all forgiveness of sins is the capstone promise of the new covenant prophesied in Jeremiah 31:31–34, which Hebrews cites to open and conclude his exposition of Jesus's priestly ministry (Heb. 8:8–12; 10:15–17). The primacy of this new covenant promise, "I will remember their sins and their lawless deeds no more" (10:17), is un- derscored by the following comment: "Where there is forgiveness of these, there is no longer any offering for sin" (10:18). Because of this forgiveness, God fulfills the other new covenant promises as well, including purified consciences (9:14)—

I will put my laws on their hearts
  and write them on their minds (10:16)—

and access to his presence for all who draw near by faith to God through Jesus (7:25; see 4:14–16; 10:19–22)—

They shall *all* know me,
  from the least of them to the greatest. (8:11)

Hebrews uses several terms to express the removal of sin's defilement from human conscience. First, Christ's death "sanctifies" (*hagiazō*) his people both decisively at the outset of their Christian pilgrimage and progressively throughout their life of persevering faith. Thus, believers "*have been sanctified* [Greek perfect aspect] through the offering of the body of Jesus Christ once for all" (10:10)—a completed accomplishment. Jesus "suffered outside the gate in order to *sanctify* the people though his own blood" (13:12). But those who *have been* sanctified are also in the process of *being sanctified*: "By a single offering he *has perfected* [Greek perfect aspect of *teleioō*] for all time those who *are being sanctified* [Greek present/progressive aspect]" (10:14).

Second, "cleanse" or "purify" (*katharizō* and its cognates) is virtually synonymous with "sanctify," as Hebrews 9:13–14 shows. Since animals' blood and ashes "sanctify" (*hagiazō*) for "purification" (*katharotēs*) of the flesh, how much more will Christ's blood "purify" (*katharizō*) our consciences. Animal deaths could not "cleanse" worshipers deeply to eliminate the consciousness of sins that troubled their defiled consciences (10:1–2). But the Son has made "purification" (*katharismos*) for sins (1:3). Through the blood of Jesus, therefore, we may draw near "with our hearts sprinkled clean [*katharos*] from an evil conscience" (10:22).

Third, the imagery of "sprinkling" (*hrantizō* and its cognates) is drawn from the law's physical ritual of applying liquid to persons or objects, symbolically removing their defilement. Water containing the ashes of a sacrificed heifer was sprinkled on individuals to transfer them from "unclean" status—excluded from the community—into "clean" status, able to rejoin the worshiping congregation (Heb. 9:13, referring to Num. 19:17–19). Believers may draw near because their hearts have been "sprinkled clean from an evil conscience" (Heb. 10:22). Therefore, by faith they now worship in the heavenly Jerusalem where they encounter Jesus and his "sprinkled [*rhantismos*] blood," which advocates for their cleansing (12:24).

Finally, through Jesus's death, worshipers are "perfected" (*teleioō*). As we have seen, in Hebrews to "be perfected" is to be permitted to enter the sanctuary of God. For Christ the sinless one, his self-sacrifice on behalf of sinful people marked his personal "perfection"—that is, his appointment by God to be high priest forever after the order of Melchizedek (see 2:10; 5:9–10; 7:28). For sin-stained humanity, *only Christ's blood,* offered without blemish, could purify so deeply as to render them acceptable to approach God in his holiness. The law and its sacrifices could not perfect defiled consciences (7:19; 9:9; 10:1). But "by a single offering [Christ] has *perfected* for all time those who are being sanctified" (10:14). Because of Christ's all-sufficient, once-for-all sacrifice, no defilement prevents their "unimpeded access to God and unbroken communion with him."[10]

The animal sacrifices and cleansing rites conducted by Aaronic priests could purify the flesh but go no deeper (9:9–10, 13). They could not remove the defilement of sin from worshipers' consciences, so they could not qualify them to enter God's presence. In contrast, Christ's offering of his body in sacrificial death achieves the sanctifying/cleansing/perfecting of worshipers' consciences, decisively and forever (9:14; 10:22). His sacrifice has "sanctified" his people "once for all" (*ephapax*) (10:10) and "for all time" (*eis to diēnikes*) (10:12, 14). The author's relentless emphasis on the "once-ness" of Jesus's sacrificial offering stands in sharp contrast to the ceaseless repetition of animal

10 F. F. Bruce, *The Epistle to the Hebrews*, NICNT, rev. ed. (Grands Rapids, MI: Eerdmans, 1990), 80.

sacrifices, redundancy that made those offerings reminders of sin, not means of sin's removal (10:2–4).

Redemption and New Covenant Inauguration

Christ's sacrifice also links his *priestly* ministry with his role as the *mediator* of the new and better covenant. Under the Mosaic covenant, Moses himself functioned as covenant mediator (Gal. 3:19–29),[11] and his brother Aaron was high priest. Hebrews teaches the convergence of these two roles, priest and covenant mediator, in Jesus. In contrast to the Levitical priests who offered gifts in the earthly sanctuary, "Christ has obtained a ministry that is as much more excellent than the old as the covenant he mediates is better, since it is enacted on better promises" (Heb. 8:6).

As we have seen, the ratification of biblical covenants over dead bodies (Gen. 15:9–11, 17–18; Jer. 34:18–20) and the sprinkling of blood at the inauguration of the Mosaic covenant (Ex. 24:8) symbolized the violent death that would befall anyone who transgressed the covenant, breaching the exclusive loyalty that it demanded (Heb. 9:16–20).[12] Hebrews explains how Christ's sacrifice both addresses the curse of the broken old covenant and inaugurates the unbreakable new covenant:

> [T]he blood of Christ, who through the eternal Spirit offered himself without blemish to God, [will] *purify our conscience* from dead works to serve the living God. Therefore he is the *mediator of a new covenant*, so that those who are called may receive the promised eternal inheritance, since *a death has occurred that redeems them* from the transgressions committed under the first covenant. (Heb. 9:14–15)

By vicariously enduring the cursed death that violators of that first covenant deserved, Christ accomplished their redemption. To redeem

---

11 Referring to Moses's role in Gal. 3:19–20, the ESV translates *mesitēs* as "intermediary," a synonym of "mediator," the term that the ESV uses to represent *mesitēs* in Hebrews (8:6; 9:15; 12:24).

12 See p. 45 for my discussion under "Sacrifice" in chap. 2.

(*lytroō*) is *to rescue and release*, whether from slavery (Ex. 6:6 LXX), from sinful behavior (Titus 2:14; 1 Pet. 1:18), or—as in Hebrews 9:15 (using the noun *apolytrōsis*)—from *liability to condemnation and punishment*. So Christ's death is the point of intersection between the old covenant and the new. By securing redemption from the curse incurred by sins committed under the first covenant, Jesus mediates the new covenant, not only inaugurating this bond but also sustaining it perpetually, guaranteeing its promises of forgiveness, heart transformation, and intimate access to God for all (7:22)—the combination of blessings that Hebrews calls "the promised eternal inheritance" (9:15).

The author's thought coincides with Paul's in Galatians 3. Christ's death accomplished redemption from the curse of the law under the first covenant:

> For all who rely on works of the law are under a curse; for it is written, "Cursed be everyone who does not abide by all things written in the Book of the Law, and do them." . . . Christ redeemed us from the curse of the law by becoming a curse for us—for it is written, "Cursed is everyone who is hanged on a tree." (Gal. 3:10, 13)[13]

And this redemption from the law's curse introduces the blessings of the new covenant: "so that in Christ Jesus the blessing of Abraham might come to the Gentiles, so that we might receive the promised Spirit through faith" (Gal. 3:14).

Sanctuary Consecration

Having shown how Christ's death fulfills the symbolism of the covenant inauguration at Sinai and provides redemption from that covenant's transgressions, our author connects the sprinkled blood by which the people were consecrated with the sprinkling used to consecrate the *ancient sanctuary and its furnishings* (Heb. 9:21–23). When it was erected, the tabernacle and its furnishings were anointed with oil,

---

13 On redemption's identification with forgiveness, see also Eph. 1:7; Col. 1:14.

as were the priests (Ex. 30:22–33; 40:9–11; Lev. 8:10–13). Hebrews, however, seems to have in mind the annual Day of Atonement, when blood was applied to "make atonement" for the altar of incense, the Most Holy Place, the whole tent of meeting, and the altar of burnt offering in the courtyard (Ex. 30:10; Lev. 16:15–19; see Ex. 29:36–37). The sanctuary needed such atonement through sprinkled blood "because of the uncleannesses of the people of Israel and because of their transgressions, all their sins" (Lev. 16:16). The rite involved the sprinkling of blood on *physical* objects; the cleansing that it symbolized focused on the *spiritual* defilement of *persons* through their sin. The intimate association, almost identification, of sinful people with the sanctuary at which they worshiped is the lesson that Hebrews draws from the use of blood to consecrate the earthly tent and its vessels: "Indeed, under the law almost everything is purified by blood, and without the shedding of blood there is no *forgiveness of sins*" (Heb. 9:22).

This identification of the sanctuary with the worshipers is probably the explanation of the surprising "how much more" reasoning that immediately follows: "Thus it was necessary for the copies of the heavenly things[14] to be purified with these rites, but the heavenly things themselves with better sacrifices than these" (9:23). If we understand "the heavenly things themselves" to refer to God's eternal dwelling place in heaven (9:11, 24), it is hard to explain why that *supremely holy* divine residence would need to be "purified" or "cleansed" (*katharizō*). R. B. Jamieson argues that by "the heavenly things" Hebrews refers to "a place of commerce between the creator and at least some of his creatures," a sanctuary that is "not of this creation (9.11), but it is not uncreated."[15]

---

14   That is, the earthly tabernacle and its furnishings. Hebrews 8:5 infers, based on God's direction to Moses, that everything related to the tabernacle be made "according to the pattern that was shown you on the mountain" (see Ex. 25:40), that the sanctuary in which Levitical priests serve was an earthly "copy and shadow" of God's true and original palace in heaven.

15   R. B. Jamieson, "Hebrews 9.23: Cult Inauguration, Yom Kippur, and the Cleansing of the Heavenly Tabernacle," *NTS* 62 (2016): 581. William L. Lane, *Hebrews 9–13*, WBC 47B (Dallas: Word, 1991), 247, reasons similarly: "The heavenly sanctuary had also become defiled by the sin of the people. . . . Sin as defilement is infectious. An individual assumes his part in the community through social relationships and cultic acts. Consequently,

This heaven, Jamieson reasons, may be defiled by creatures' sins and need cleansing by Christ's blood, just as Israel's high priest cleansed its earthly replica, the tabernacle, with its ark and its altar (Lev. 16:15–20). Scripture does refer to the presence of evil creatures in God's heavenly court. Jamieson offers only Job 15:15 as biblical support, but he might have cited Job 1–2; Zechariah 3:1; and Ephesians 6:12—and perhaps Luke 10:18 and Revelation 12:7–12 (see also 1 Kings 22:19–23). Typically, however, such defiling creatures (Satan and other evil spirits) are not said to be cleansed but rather to be rebuked by God or expelled from his presence.

Hebrews explains the use of blood to sprinkle, and thereby purify, the earthly tent and its vessels, with the rationale that "without the shedding of blood there is *no forgiveness of sins*" (Heb. 9:22). Forgiveness of sins is not a ceremonial concept but rather an interpersonal and spiritual transaction that pertains to guilty humans' relationship to God. That connection between cleansing by blood and forgiveness of sins favors the view that "the heavenly things" now purified by Christ's better sacrifice should be understood as believing worshipers.[16] The plural expression "the heavenly things themselves" (*auta . . . ta epourania*) in Hebrews 9:23 corresponds to the tent and its vessels that are their copies. The slight difference in terminology between this expression and the singular "heaven itself" (*auton ton ouranon*), which Christ has entered (9:24), suggests that the objects

---

the effects of his defilement contaminate society, . . . the sanctuary where God met with his people, . . . and even the inanimate vessels used in the cultus. . . . That the effects of sin also extend to the heavenly world is a corollary of the solidarity that the writer perceives between ultimate reality in heaven and its reflection on earth." Thomas R. Schreiner, *Hebrews*, BTCP (Nashville: Holman Reference, 2013), 283, rejects the idea that "the heavenly things" refer to the people of God, but he also denies that there is "any notion here that the heavenly places are defiled and literally need cleansing. . . . [T]he author often writes typologically when citing the OT, and thus the reference to the cleansing of the heavenly places should not be understood literally or univocally but analogically."

16 For example, Bruce, *Hebrews*, 228–29; Hugh Montefiore, *The Epistle to the Hebrews*, HNTC (San Francisco: Harper and Row, 1964), 160; Harold W. Attridge, *The Epistle to the Hebrews*, Hermeneia (Philadelphia: Fortress, 1989), 261–62.

of Christ's purifying sacrifice belong to the heavenly sphere in which he now ministers, while avoiding the implication that human sin has defiled the eternal dwelling place of God. Elsewhere Hebrews draws so close a connection between sanctuary and worshipers—equating believers with God's "house" (3:6)—that here the author can speak of those worshipers as "heavenly things." They properly belong to God's true sanctuary and confidently approach his throne of grace, since their consciences are cleansed by the blood of Christ (9:14; 10:19–22; see 12:28; 13:15–16).

Intercession

Hebrews connects Jesus's priestly office with his ministry of prayer on behalf of sinners in the presence of God. Because Jesus is a priest forever (7:20–21), "he holds his priesthood permanently, because he continues forever" (7:24). His permanent tenure as high priest, in turn, means that "he is able to save to the uttermost those who draw near to God through him, since *he always lives to make intercession for them*" (7:25).

On the one hand, it is striking that the Old Testament most frequently associates *intercession*—prayer to God on behalf of others—not with priests but with Abraham (Gen. 20:7, 17–18), Moses as covenant mediator (e.g., Ex. 8:28–31; 33:12–23; Num. 21:7), prophets such as Samuel and Jeremiah (1 Sam. 12:19–23; Jer. 42:1–6), and kings such as Solomon and Hezekiah (1 Kings 8:22–53; 2 Kings 19:15–19). Admittedly, Aaron the high priest placed the Lord's name on the Israelites in his threefold benediction (Num. 6:22–27), but in the Hebrew Scriptures instances of prayer spoken by priests on the people's behalf are rare (note the prayer of confession by Ezra the priest in Ezra 9:5–15).

On the other hand, the priests did intercede for the people by ministering in God's sanctuary, the focal point of God's presence on earth and the site toward which needy Israelites and foreigners were to direct their petitions, trusting that the Lord would "listen in heaven," his true "dwelling place," and answer (1 Kings 8:30; see also 8:34, 36, 39,

43, 45, 49–50). Among the priests' daily duties was offering incense on the altar in the Holy Place (Ex. 30:7–8). Those incense offerings accompanied and symbolized the prayers of worshipers (Ps. 141:2; Luke 1:10–13; Rev. 5:8; 8:3–4). By such *actions*, then, priests offered intercession for the people.

Especially on the Day of Atonement, the actions of the high priest expressed intercession for the forgiveness of his fellow Israelites. The slaying of the bull and the goat were the preparatory acts, not the climax, of the atonement rite. The crucial moment was when the high priest carried the blood into the Most Holy Place and sprinkled it on the atonement cover (*kapporet*) of the ark of the covenant (Lev. 16:15). The high priest's vestments bore the names of Israel's tribes engraved on precious stones, both on the ephod that rested on his shoulders and on the breastpiece that covered his heart (Ex. 28:9–12, 17–22, 29). The tribal names on the stones symbolized the reality that the high priest approached God's throne as the representative of the people of God, bearing sacrificial blood and interceding for their forgiveness.

This climactic event of the Day of Atonement, the high priest's entry into the Most Holy Place "with blood not his own" (Heb. 9:25), is the paradigm in which new covenant believers are to understand the present priestly ministry of Jesus on our behalf. Jesus "suffered outside the gate," shedding his blood on earth to sanctify his people (13:12). Then he was raised from the dead and "passed through the heavens" (4:14), entering "once for all into the [uncreated, heavenly] holy places . . . by means of his own blood, thus securing an eternal redemption" (9:12). The ongoing presentation of that priceless blood, symbolized by Aaron's sprinkling of blood on the atonement cover in enacted petition for forgiveness, constitutes the intercession that Christ our ever-living high priest offers on behalf of his own (7:25; see Rom. 8:34).[17]

---

17 Since Jesus is the sympathetic high priest who knows temptation from personal experience and can help those undergoing temptation (2:17–18; 4:14–16), his intercession extends from his petition for his people's forgiveness to embrace all their spiritual needs. From Christ's high priestly prayer in John 17, we have reason to expect that, as our living and ascended intercessor, he continues to ask the Father to grant us unity and perseverance through the power of the Spirit.

Access and Worship

The purpose of God's covenant with humanity is worship, in which his people draw near to him to extol his glory and receive his mercy and grace (4:16; see 10:19–25). Appropriately, therefore, the quotation in Hebrews of Jeremiah's new covenant promise (8:8–13) is surrounded by the theme of sanctuary, the meeting place of God with his people (8:1–5; 9:1–6). Among the "better promises" of the new covenant (8:6) are

> They shall all know me,
>> from the least of them to the greatest.
> For I will be merciful toward their iniquities,
>> and I will remember their sins no more. (8:11–12)

Jesus's sacrifice, by fulfilling the final promise (forgiveness), established the basis for the penultimate promise (that all may know God), which Hebrews elaborates in terms of *access for all* to worship the Lord in his holy presence.

The opening of the Most Holy Place was not the experience of ordinary Israelites under the Mosaic covenant. The Levitical priests represented Israel's whole worshiping community as they entered the Lord's sanctuary to minister on behalf of their kinfolk in the other tribes. But the severe restrictions controlling access to the tabernacle (only Levitical priests could enter the Holy Place and only the high priest could enter the Most Holy Place) meant that the Levitical-Aaronic priests' role as gatekeepers into God's presence was largely *negative and exclusionary*. The Levites' assignment, like that of the cherubim at Eden's gateway (Gen. 3:24), was to guard God's holy dwelling against trespassers who would defile the sanctuary (Num. 1:53; 3:7–8). When Israel set up camp in the wilderness, three Levite clans pitched tents on three sides of the tabernacle, and the tents of the priests (Aaron and his sons with Moses) stood on the fourth side, "before the tent of meeting toward the sunrise, . . . guarding the sanctuary itself, to protect the people of Israel" (Num. 3:38; see 18:1–5). Outside this protective, insulating perimeter of Levitical and priestly tents, Israel's remaining twelve tribes encamped. So Levitical-Aaronic priests functioned as gatekeepers to the courts of the Lord by banning all other tribes from access to the tent of meeting, excluding defiled persons from the sanctuary courtyard, and conducting rites by which unclean individuals could be pronounced cleansed and readmitted to Israel's worshiping community (Lev. 12–15; see Deut. 24:8; Luke 5:12–14). On the whole, although Aaronic priests offered sacrifices and interceded on behalf of fellow Israelites, their mission had more to do with protecting the Lord's holiness from defilement and protecting unclean people from God's consuming purity than with welcoming God's needy people into his presence.

By contrast, as mediator of the new covenant and great high priest, Christ has now entered "the inner place behind the curtain" as our "forerunner" (Heb. 6:19–20) so that all who trust in him can approach God's throne of grace with confidence:

Since then we have *a great high priest* who has passed through the heavens, Jesus, the Son of God, let us hold fast our confession. For we do not have a high priest who is unable to sympathize with our weaknesses, but one who in every respect has been tempted as we are, yet without sin. Let us then *with confidence draw near* to the throne of grace, that we may receive mercy and find grace to help in time of need. (Heb. 4:14–16)

As our great high priest, Jesus is no less zealous for the consuming holiness of the living God (10:21; 12:29). But he has offered the propitiating sacrifice that removes the defilement of our sins (2:17). His blood, offered without blemish to God, has purified (9:14), sanctified (10:10), and perfected for all time those who approach God through him (10:14). With consciences cleansed, they may now serve the living God in his presence. Hebrews does not describe the recipients as "a kingdom of priests" (Ex. 19:6), language that is applied to the new covenant church elsewhere in the New Testament (see 1 Pet. 2:5, 9;

Rev. 1:6; 5:10; 20:6). But the author's articulation of the priestly privilege that now belongs to *all* believers through Christ makes the same ecclesiological point.

The access to God's presence that Jesus grants as the new covenant's mediator and great high priest is not only *broader*—embracing all God's people—but also *higher*. Christ ushers believers not into a tent on earth but into the heavenly Most Holy Place, of which the earthly sanctuary was merely a copy and shadow. The exhortation that opens the discussion of Jesus's priestly ministry (Heb. 4:14–16) speaks of drawing near to God's throne of grace. The corresponding exhortation amplifies that *priestly privilege* of access to God's sanctuary and approach to God's presence:

> Therefore, brothers, since we have *confidence to enter* the holy places by the blood of Jesus, by the new and living way that he opened for us through the curtain, that is, through his flesh, and since we have *a great priest* over the house of God, let us *draw near with a true heart in full assurance of faith*, with our hearts sprinkled clean from an evil conscience and our bodies washed with pure water. (10:19–22)

The holy places that we now enter through the curtain are the heavenly sanctuary that Christ "entered once for all" at his ascension, when he passed through "the greater and more perfect tent (not made with hands, that is, not of this creation" (9:11–12). In that heavenly sanctuary he has taken his seat at God's right hand, having completed his sacrificial ministry (8:1–2; 10:11–13). Through his sacrifice and intercession, all believers have access to the true and eternal Most Holy Place where he serves as our mediator and representative.

Even though Christians live and suffer on earth, they also *may and do* enter the heavenly sanctuary, where our high priest ever lives to intercede for us. On the one hand, we are waiting for the everlasting "city that is to come" (13:14). On the other, *even now* we "have come" (*proselēlythate*, perfect aspect of *proserchomai*) to the city of the living God, the heavenly Jerusalem, joining celebrating angels and perfected saints in the presence of God through the blood of Jesus (12:22–24). This striking claim does not refer to mystical experience or ecstatic vision. Rather, congregations that assemble in Jesus's name to stimulate each other's loving obedience (10:24–25) and to "exhort one another every day" (3:13) are genuinely participating *by faith* (the proof of things unseen, 11:1) in the worship taking place in God's heavenly sanctuary.

As priests who have been granted access to God's presence by grace, believers should "offer to God acceptable [*euarestōs*] worship"—adoration and service that pleases him—"with reverence and awe" (12:28). The sufficiency and finality of Christ's once-for-all sacrifice renders obsolete the law's entire system of animal sacrifices (10:5–10). No further bloodshed is needed to atone for sins (10:18). Yet the ever-widening circle of priests still has "sacrifices" (*thysias*) to offer that are "pleasing [*euaresteō*] to God" (13:16). These offerings are, first, "a sacrifice of praise [*thysian aineseōs*], the fruit of lips that acknowledge [or "confess," *homologeō*][18] his name" (13:15). The expression "sacrifice of praise" is probably drawn from Psalm 49 LXX (50 ET), which, like Psalm 40, expresses God's displeasure with Israel's animal sacrifices. More pleasing in God's sight, says the psalmist, are "a sacrifice of praise" (*thysian aineseōs*, Ps. 49:14 LXX), spoken expressions of thanksgiving, vows fulfilled, humble petition, and faithful obedience (Ps. 49:12–15, 24 LXX [50:12–15, 24 ET]).

Hebrews 13:15 applies to this spoken "sacrifice" another expression drawn from the Old Testament, "the fruit of lips" (*karpon cheileōn*). In Hosea 14:1–2 (14:2–3 MT and LXX), the prophet counsels sinful Israel to return to the Lord, bringing words of repentance and promising to respond to God's forgiving grace with "the fruit of our lips" (*karpon cheileōn hēmōn*, Hos. 14:3 LXX).[19] In Hebrews, "the fruit of

---

18 The rendering "confess" (CSB) is preferable to "acknowledge" for the reasons given in the following discussion.

19 The Hebrew Masoretic Text has "We will pay the bulls [*parim*] of our lips" (Hos. 14:3 MT), which the ESV interprets, "We will pay with bulls / the vows of our lips." (14:2). The LXX *karpon cheileōn* apparently reflects a Hebrew original that read, "We will pay the fruit [*pari*] of our lips."

lips" is to be offered in grateful response (Heb. 13:15) to Jesus's sanctifying suffering (13:12) and to God's promise of "the city that is to come" (13:14). Moreover, our lips "confess [*homologeō*] his name." Confession—that is, spoken, corporate affirmation of trust in Jesus and loyalty to him—is a common motif in Hebrews. Jesus Christ is "the high priest of our confession [*homologia*]" (3:1). The exhortations that introduce and conclude the sermon's central discussion of Christ's priesthood (4:14–16; 10:19–25) urge in almost identical terms: "Let us hold fast [our/the] confession [*homologia*]" (4:14; 10:23).[20] In both exhortations this adherence to the confession is linked to the call to "draw near" to God in prayer and in the worshiping community (4:16; 10:22), "stir[ring] up one another, . . . not neglecting to meet together" (10:24–25). Our "sacrifice of praise" is the fruit of lips that *declare together* (*homologeō*) our hope and our trust in the God who faithfully keeps his promises.

Believers who have been "perfected" by Christ's sacrifice to serve in God's presence also worship through other sacrifices: "Do not neglect to do good and to share what you have [*koinōnia*], for such sacrifices [*thusia*] are pleasing [*euraresteō*] to God" (13:16). The original audience had a history of love and service to the saints (6:10) and had demonstrated solidarity with fellow believers who suffered public humiliation and other forms of persecution (10:32–34). Now they must continue to "offer to God acceptable worship" (12:28) by maintaining brotherly love, extending hospitality to strangers, and reaching out to prisoners (13:1–3). Generous sharing (*koinōnia*) with Christian brothers and sisters in need was a hallmark of the early church in Jerusalem (Acts 2:42–45; 4:32–35). The church at Philippi consistently contributed toward the apostle Paul's labors, and he gratefully acknowledged their donations as "partnership [*koinōnia*] with me in giving and receiving" (Phil. 4:15), even referring to it in sacrificial imagery: "a fragrant offering, a sacrifice [*thusian*] acceptable and pleas-

---

20 The ESV uses "hold fast" to reflect the Greek verbs *krateō* (4:14) and *katechō* (10:23), which are synonymous in these contexts.

ing [*euareston*] to God" (Phil. 4:18; see also 1 Pet. 2:5). God receives and approves service to the saints as worship offered to himself (see Matt. 25:31–40).

Finally, since Hebrews calls attention to Jesus's priestly role as the ever-living intercessor (Heb. 7:23–25), now that Christ has opened access to all believers, they must approach God's throne not only to receive mercy and grace for themselves (4:16) but also to intercede for each other. The author appeals for their priestly intercession for himself: "Pray for us, for we are sure that we have a clear conscience, desiring to act honorably in all things. I urge you the more earnestly to do this in order that I may be restored to you the sooner" (13:18–19).

The new covenant priests, "from the least of them to the greatest" (8:11), now perfected once-for-all by Christ's sacrifice, enjoy access to God's heavenly sanctuary by faith. Through Jesus's mediation, they offer "acceptable worship, with reverence and awe" (12:28), with their lips speaking "a sacrifice of praise" (13:15) and with their hands performing deeds of compassion and generosity toward others, sacrifices that our God receives with pleasure (13:16).

Conclusion

Central to Jesus's ministry as high priest and to his mission as mediator of the new covenant prophesied by Jeremiah is his self-offering in death as the once-for-all, wrath-propitiating, conscience-purifying sacrifice for sinners. He "offered himself without blemish to God" (9:14), laying down his life "outside the gate" (13:12), taking up his life again, and ascending "through the heavens" (4:14) to present his shed blood before God, "the judge of all" (12:23–24). By his completed and all-sufficient sacrifice and through his ceaseless intercession, Jesus secures "eternal redemption" (9:12) and everlasting forgiveness for all who approach God through him (10:17–18). Since his unique high priestly ministry has "perfected" the conscience of believers (10:14), his blood has opened access for all of them, "from the least of them to the greatest" (8:11), into the heavenly Most Holy Place, where Christ now sits enthroned at the right hand of the majesty, awaiting the sub-jection of all his enemies.

Meanwhile, God's redeemed people on earth eagerly await the re-appearance of their great high priest from the heavenly sanctuary, anticipating the consummation of their salvation that his return will bring (9:28). Their consciences cleansed by his blood, they draw near the throne of grace to receive mercy and help for their wilderness pilgrimage. And they offer worship that pleases God, holding fast to their confession, declaring God's praise, stimulating each other to love and good deeds, and encouraging each other daily to persevering trust.

Persevering Faith through Congregational Solidarity

Run with endurance.

HEBREWS 12:1

Because Jesus Is Better, Endure in Faith

As we have seen, Hebrews is a "word of exhortation" (Heb. 13:22), an early Jewish-Christian sermon in which pastoral application is interwoven with rich theological discussion. Consistent with the author's homiletical genre, as his case for Jesus's superiority unfolds, each theological theme leads into a hortatory section that applies the truth just presented (2:1–4; 3:7–4:13; 4:14–16; 5:11–6:12; 10:19–31; 12:1–17, 25–29; 13:1–17). These hortatory passages, far from being sidebars or interruptions in the theological argument, express the objectives toward which the didactic discussions are driving.

These hortatory sections return again and again to *one specific response* (expressed in a variety of ways) that the various dimensions of Jesus's superiority should evoke from the hearers: they must *endure* in *faith, holding fast* their shared confession by *encouraging* each other and *drawing near* to God in worship and prayer.[1] So this sermon's theological

---

1 As Hebrews draws to a close, the author also issues a succession of brief directives on a wider variety of ethical issues: brotherly love, hospitality to strangers, compassion for

argument for Christ's superiority is directed toward *two interrelated pastoral objectives*: to motivate hearers to *persevere in trusting* God's promises and to *encourage* one another's endurance in faith.

These exhortations to enduring faith are expressed not only in *positive encouragements* ("let us . . ."; "we must . . .") but also in *negative warnings* ("lest . . ."; "see to it that . . . not") and conditional clauses ("if we . . ."):

- "Therefore we must pay much closer attention to what we have heard, *lest* we drift away from it" (2:1).
- "Consider Jesus, the apostle and high priest of our confession. . . . We are his house, *if indeed* we hold fast our confidence and our boasting in our hope" (3:1, 6).
- "Take care, brothers, *lest* there be in any of you an evil, unbelieving heart, leading you to fall away from the living God. But exhort one another every day" (3:12–13).
- "Therefore, while the promise of entering his rest still stands, let us fear *lest* any of you should seem to have failed to reach it" (4:1).
- "*Let us* hold fast our confession. . . . *Let us* then with confidence draw near to the throne of grace" (4:14, 16).
- "Therefore *let us* leave the elementary doctrine of Christ and go on to maturity" (6:1).
- "And we desire each one of you to show the same earnestness to have the full assurance of hope until the end, so that *you may not be* sluggish, but imitators of those who through faith and patience inherit the promises" (6:11–12).
- "Therefore, brothers, since we have confidence to enter the holy places by the blood of Jesus . . . *let us* draw near with a true heart

---

prisoners, sexual purity and marital fidelity, financial contentment, generosity toward the needy, and respect for leaders (13:1–17). So the author's conclusion stylistically resembles New Testament Epistles (see, e.g., Phil. 4:2–9; 1 Thess. 5:12–21; Jude 20–21). Also, the exhortation in Heb. 12:1–17, which belongs to the body of the sermon and therefore highlights *enduring faith and hope*, also includes other specific ethical directions: to pursue peace and holiness and to shun Esau's example of sensuality and self-indulgent disregard for God's covenant promises (12:16–17).

in full assurance of faith. . . . *Let us* hold fast the confession of our hope without wavering. . . . And *let us* consider how to stir up one another to love and good works, not neglecting to meet together" (10:19, 22–25).

- "Therefore do not throw away your confidence, which has a great reward. For you have need of endurance, so that when you have done the will of God, you may receive what is promised" (10:35–36).
- "*Let us* also lay aside every weight . . . and *let us* run with endurance the race that is set before us, looking to Jesus" (12:1).
- "Have you forgotten the exhortation that addresses you as sons? 'My son, do not regard lightly the discipline of the Lord, / nor be weary when reproved by him'" (12:5).
- "*See to it* that *no one* fails to obtain the grace of God; that no 'root of bitterness' springs up and causes trouble, and by it many become defiled" (12:15).
- "*See* that you do *not* refuse him who is speaking" (12:25).
- "Therefore *let us* be grateful . . . and thus *let us* offer to God acceptable worship, with reverence and awe" (12:28).

The sobering *warnings* target the same danger from various angles. Hearers must not drift away, fall away, fail to reach God's rest, remain immature and sluggish, throw away their confidence, shrink back, fail to obtain God's grace, or refuse the Lord who speaks from heaven. The heartening *exhortations* are also diverse: pay closer attention, consider Jesus, hold fast the confession and hope, encourage each other, draw near to God's throne of grace, move toward maturity, imitate earlier believers, retain confidence and receive God's promises, run with endurance (eyes fixed on Jesus), receive God's painful discipline as proof of his love, listen receptively, and worship thankfully and acceptably. Together, the warnings and the exhortations sing the same song in harmony: run with endurance the race of faith.

Hebrews reinforces its exhortations to forward-focused faith with both *negative and positive examples* from Israel's history recorded in the Old Testament. Negatively, we must beware the shameful history of Israel's wilderness generation that escaped Egyptian slavery, saw God's deeds in the desert, and heard his voice but responded with hardened, unbelieving hearts (Heb. 3–4, expounding Ps. 95). Positively, the hearers must become "imitators of those who through faith and patience inherit the promises" (6:12). This "cloud of witnesses" (12:1) who speak from the Old Testament, bearing witness to God's faithfulness, includes Abraham (6:11–18) and the other patriarchs (11:8–22); their predecessors in faith, including Abel, Enoch, and Noah (11:3–7); their successors in faith, including Moses, Joshua, and Rahab; and others too numerous for their stories to be retold (11:23–12:1). To these ancient examples we now turn, following the order laid out by Hebrews: the negative example of the unbelieving wilderness generation (3:7–4:13), followed by the positive examples whom God commended for their faith (11:2, 39).

The Negative Example of Israel's Faithless Apostasy

In chapter 1 we saw that Hebrews 3:7–4:13 presents the experience of Israel's wilderness generation as a paradigm by which new covenant believers should interpret their own pilgrimage through life on earth. Hebrews draws four parallels between the wilderness generation and the situation confronting the Jewish Christians to whom this sermon was addressed: (1) as covenant communities, both had experienced God's redemptive interventions *in the past*, (2) both were addressed by God's voice, speaking good news *in the present*, (3) both received a promise of entering God's rest *in the future*, and (4) both were undergoing testing as homeless aliens in a hostile environment. For all four parallels, there are contrasts as well as similarities between the wilderness generation and the audience of Hebrews. With respect to the first three, the contrast is incremental, between "good" and "better." The redemptive liberation now achieved by Christ transcends the exodus from Egypt (2:14–16). The salvation spoken by the Lord Jesus transcends the law administered by angels at Sinai (2:1–4). The heavenly country and the everlasting city to come transcend the "rest" of occupying earthly Canaan (4:8–11; 11:10, 13–16; 13:14). For the fourth parallel, however, the contrast is antithetical, between opposites: the hard-hearted unbelief of (almost) the entire wilderness generation *must not be imitated* by anyone in the Jewish-Christian congregation that Hebrews addresses (3:12–14; 3:19–4:2, 6, 11).

People on pilgrimage through hostile terrain, surrounded by all-too-visible dangers and deprivations, must "walk by faith, not by sight" (2 Cor 5:7). But that walk of persistent faith—steady trust in God's voice, which promises things not yet seen—did not characterize the wilderness generation, although they had experienced miraculous liberation from Egypt and God's miraculous provision and protection in the Sinai desert. Ten spies returned from Canaan with a faithless report that filled the Israelites with terror. Only Joshua and Caleb called their countrymen to trust their faithful and almighty God:

> The land, which we passed through to spy it out, is an exceedingly good land. If the Lord delights in us, he will bring us into this land and give it to us, a land that flows with milk and honey. Only do not rebel [LXX: *mē apostatai ginesthe,* "do not become apostates"] against the Lord. And do not fear the people of the land. . . . Their protection is removed from them, and the Lord is with us; do not fear them." (Num. 14:7–9)

For their courageous counsel, Joshua and Caleb were threatened with death by their unbelieving countrymen, until the Lord himself appeared in glory and spoke:

> How long will this people despise me? And how long will they not believe [LXX: *ou pisteuousin*] in me, in spite of all the signs that I have done among them? . . . Truly, as I live, and as all the earth shall be filled with the glory of the Lord, none of the men who *have seen my glory and my signs* that I did in Egypt and in the wilderness, and

yet have put me to the test [LXX: *epeirasan me*] these ten times and have not obeyed my voice, shall see the land that I swore to give to their fathers. (Num. 14:11, 21–23)

Two elements in this account illuminate the author's commentary on Psalm 95. First, Caleb tells the Israelites that to refuse to enter the land is to "rebel against" or "apostatize"[2] from God, while the Lord calls it unbelief (*ou pisteuousin*). Hebrews likewise links unbelief to apostasy: "Take care, brothers, lest there be in any of you an evil, unbelieving [*apistias*] heart, leading you to fall away [*apostēnai*][3] from the living God" (Heb. 3:12). Hebrews also uses "unbelief" and "disobedience" interchangeably in diagnosing the wilderness generation's failure: "They were unable to enter because of *unbelief* [*apistian*]" (3:19), and they "failed to enter because of *disobedience* [*apeitheia*]" (4:6, see 3:18; 4:11). Disbelieving God's promises involves disregard of his commands and high treason against his person.

Second, the fact that the wilderness generation had witnessed God's works of rescue and provision compounded their guilt for failing to trust the divine champion. Psalm 95:9 (94:9 LXX), cited in Hebrews 3:9, picks up this theme:

Your fathers put me to the test
  and *saw my works* for forty years.

Hebrews likewise implies that witnessing the events of the exodus made those wilderness wanderers more culpable for their unbelief:

For who were those who heard and yet rebelled? Was it not *all those who left Egypt led by Moses*? And with whom was he provoked for forty years? Was it not with those who sinned, whose bodies fell in

---

2 In Num. 14:9 LXX, "do not become apostates [*apostatai*]" contains the noun-cognate of the verb used in Heb. 3:12: *aphistēmi*, meaning "desert, fall away, become apostate." See "ἀφίστημι," in BAGD 126.

3 Aorist active infinitive of *aphistēmi*.

the wilderness? And to whom did he swear that they would not enter his rest, but to those who were disobedient? (3:16–18)

The wilderness generation had seen plagues sent on their Egyptian oppressors, had crossed the sea on dry ground, had been protected by the cloud of glory, had drunk water from the rock and eaten manna from heaven. Yet all except Caleb and Joshua refused to believe that the Lord could bestow the homeland that he had promised. So, after forty years in the wasteland, their "bodies fell in the wilderness" (3:17).

Hebrews draws from the wilderness generation's horrible example the sobering lesson that it is possible to *belong to a community* that experiences magnificent displays of God's redemptive grace and hears God speak good news but to forfeit blessing through unbelief. The division between believers and unbelievers *within* the community that hears God's good news is the point of Hebrews 4:2. The ESV, reflecting the Greek text most widely attested in early and reliable manuscripts,[4] reads, "For good news came to us just as to them, but the message they heard did not benefit them, because *they were not united* by faith with those who listened." William Lane argues rightly that "those who listened" refers to Caleb and Joshua, "who listened to the promise of God and regarded it as certain."[5] Hebrews will drive home the point that "by faith" (*pistei*) the ancients acted on God's promises and received his approbation (11:4, 5, 7, 8, 9, 11, 17, 20, 21, 22, 23, 24, 27, 28, 29, 30, 31).

This distinction between being *a member of the community* in which God's redemptive power is at work, on the one hand, and being *a beneficiary by faith* of his saving grace, on the other, is what theologians

---

4   Most early and reliable Greek manuscripts contain a masculine *plural* participle in Heb. 4:2, reflected in "united with," indicating that "they" (namely, the Israelites who disbelieved, disobeyed, and died in the desert) "were not united [*synkekerasmenous*] by faith with those who listened." A less widespread textual tradition, including other reliable Greek manuscripts, has a masculine *singular* participle, yielding the meaning that "the *message* [*logos*] they heard . . . was not united with faith in the hearers" (namely, the majority who heard God's voice but did not believe).

5   William L. Lane, *Hebrews 1–8*, WBC 47A (Dallas: Word, 1991), 98.

describe as the distinction between the "visible" church and the "invisible" church.[6] A classic Reformation confession, the Westminster Confession of Faith (1646), states,

1. The catholic or universal church which is *invisible*, consists of *the whole number of the elect*, that have been, are, or shall be gathered into one, under Christ the Head thereof; and is the spouse, the body, the fulness of Him who filleth all in all.
2. The *visible* church, which is also catholic or universal under the gospel (not confined to one nation, as before under the law), consists of *all those throughout the world that profess the true religion; and of their children.*[7]

Influenced by Paul's discussion of Abraham's sons Ishmael and Isaac in Romans 9, this confession traces the membership of the invisible church back to its source in God's sovereign election. The implication is that the boundaries of this eternally and redemptively blessed number (the invisible church, Abraham's true offspring) are not conterminous with the membership of the visible church. The visible church is composed of those who *profess* faith along with their children, but it may include those who lack true faith.

Hebrews views the distinction between invisible and visible church from the perspective of the fruit of God's electing grace, namely, faith. Recognizing that God alone infallibly discerns the thoughts of the human heart (Heb. 4:12–13), our author counsels his hearers not to presume on their external identification with a Christian congregation but to embrace God's promises in personal, transformative, and persevering trust. Just as many who left Egypt with Moses failed to embrace God's good news in living and lasting faith, so also members of the new covenant community may be at risk of "fall[ing] away from the living God" (3:12). For this reason, the hearers must "exhort

---

6   Edmund P. Clowney, *The Church*, Contours of Christian Theology (Downers Grove, IL: InterVarsity Press, 1995), 108–11.
7   Westminster Confession of Faith 25.1–2 (emphasis added).

one another every day . . . that none of you may be hardened by the deceitfulness of sin" (3:13).

In fact, under the new covenant mediated by Christ, the stakes are even higher than for Israel's wilderness generation. The magnified grace that the Son has secured by his incarnation, sacrifice, and everlasting priestly intercession compounds the dire consequences for anyone who, having witnessed his work among his people, repudiates his redemptive reign and turns away.[8] Three passages—Hebrews 2:1–4; 6:4–8; 10:26–31—issue this warning against apostasy.

Hebrews 2:1–4, drawing application from the superiority of the Son to angels shown in the catena of Old Testament citations (1:4–14), reasons "from lesser to greater" that justly severe sanctions for violating the law "declared by angels" (2:2) signal that *no escape is possible* "if we neglect such a great salvation" (2:3) now revealed through the divine Son. The new covenant salvation message "was declared at first by the Lord"[9] (2:3) and then attested by apostolic witnesses who heard him.[10] As they testified, God confirmed their message through his own witness (*synepimartyrountos*), in "signs and wonders and various miracles [*dynamesin*, "acts of power"] and by gifts [or, better, "distributions"][11] of the Holy Spirit" (Heb. 2:4). Acts shows the apostles' testimony confirmed by the Spirit's role as divine witness through his miraculous signs (Acts 14:3; 5:32). For the Israelites, God's plagues, parting of the sea, pillar of cloud and fire, and provision of water and bread bore witness to Moses's mediatorial authority as God's prophet. So now to the hearers of Hebrews, the Holy Spirit's signs and acts of power (*dynameis*) have confirmed the apostolic gospel. Thus, there can be no escape for those who neglect such a message, confirmed by such a glorious divine speaker (2:3).

8 This redemptive-historical escalation of covenant sanctions was introduced above in chap. 3.
9 "Lord" (*kyrios*) is picked up from the citation of Ps. 102 (Heb. 1:10).
10 See Acts 1:8, 21–22; 2:32; 3:15; 4:33; 10:39–41; 13:31.
11 *Merismois* focuses specifically on the separation (see Heb. 4:12) or diversified apportionment of manifestations (thus, "distributions") of the Spirit among God's various spokespersons (Acts 2:2–4, 17–18; 5:12–16; 8:5–8; 2 Cor. 12:12).

The testimony of the Holy Spirit through miracles—the "powers of the age to come" (*dynameis mellontos aiōnos*)—reappears in 6:5 in the second warning against apostasy (Heb. 6:4–8). The summons to press on to maturity (6:1) is reinforced by a sobering declaration: "It is impossible" (*adynaton*) (6:4) for those who, having experienced God's gracious benefits, "have fallen away" (*parapesontas*) (6:6) to be restored again to repentance. The list of divine blessings from which apostates fall away into irremediable condemnation is impressive: they have been "enlightened, . . . have tasted the heavenly gift, and have shared in the Holy Spirit, and have tasted the goodness of the word of God and the powers of the age to come" (6:4–5). This experience of God's gracious gifts seems at first glance to describe people savingly united to Christ by faith, through the regenerating power of the Holy Spirit.[12] These blessings are so great that, when our author envisions the possibility that anyone so blessed might fall away, he may seem to doubt the assurances of God's invincible preserving grace that appear elsewhere in the New Testament:

My sheep hear my voice, and I know them, and they follow me. I give them eternal life, and they will *never perish*, and *no one will snatch them out of my hand.* My Father, who has given them to me, is greater than all, and *no one is able to snatch them out of the Father's hand.* (John 10:27–29)

For those whom he *foreknew* he also *predestined* to be conformed to the image of his Son. . . . And those whom he *predestined* he also *called,* and those whom he *called* he also *justified,* and those whom he *justified* he also *glorified.* . . . *Who shall separate us from the love of Christ?* Shall tribulation, or distress, or persecution, or famine, or

12 Lane, *Hebrews 1–8,* 141–42, writes, "Together, the clauses describe vividly the reality of the experience of personal salvation enjoyed by the Christians addressed. The Holy Spirit had not only formed the community but was bringing it to eschatological fulfillment. . . . If those who have enjoyed a full and authentic Christian experience should then fall away, a renewal to repentance is impossible (v. 6)." See also Thomas R. Schreiner, *Hebrews,* BTCP (Nashville: Holman Reference, 2013), 180–89, though he argues that those who are elect will not fall away (469–71).

nakedness, or danger, or sword? . . . No, in all these things we are more than conquerors through him who loved us. For I am sure that *neither death nor life, nor angels nor rulers, nor things present nor things to come, nor powers, nor height nor depth, nor anything else in all creation, will be able to separate us from the love of God in Christ Jesus our Lord.* (Rom. 8:29–30, 35, 37–39)

And I am sure of this, that he who began a good work in you *will bring it to completion at the day of Jesus Christ.* (Phil. 1:6)

Blessed be the God and Father of our Lord Jesus Christ! According to his great mercy, he has caused us to be born again to a living hope through the resurrection of Jesus Christ from the dead, to an inheritance that is imperishable, undefiled, and unfading, kept in heaven for you, who *by God's power are being guarded through faith* for a salvation ready to be revealed in the last time. (1 Pet. 1:3–5)

In fact, Hebrews itself affirms the sufficiency of Christ's sacrifice to secure *eternal* salvation for those who trust him:

Consequently, he is able to *save to the uttermost* those who draw near to God through him. (Heb. 7:25)

He entered once for all into the holy places, not by means of the blood of goats and calves but by means of his own blood, thus securing an *eternal redemption.* (9:12)

And by [God's] will *we have been sanctified* through the offering of the body of Jesus Christ *once for all.* . . . For by a single offering he has *perfected for all time* those who are being sanctified. (10:10, 14)

Could our author actually envision the possibility that those for whom Christ has secured "eternal redemption" would fall away into a state of rebellious unbelief *from which there is no possibility of return*?

If, however, we recall the author's interpretation of the new covenant community's experience *through the paradigm of Israel's wilderness generation,* this suggests an understanding of the divine benefits in 6:4–5 that does not contradict the biblical evidence for the perseverance of God's elect through God's preserving power.[13] Just as all the Israelites heard God's voice in the wilderness (3:7; 4:1–2), so also the listeners of Hebrews heard the message of salvation spoken first by the Lord and then conveyed by the apostles (2:3). This congregation had been "enlightened" (10:32) and "tasted the goodness of the word of God" (6:5)—which is "the heavenly gift" (6:4) since Christ now speaks from heaven (12:25)—when they first heard the good news (4:2). As the Israelites saw God's works (3:9, 16), so also this congregation saw God add his own testimony to the apostolic witness through miracles (*dynamesin*) performed by the Holy Spirit (2:4), signaling the dawn of the "age to come" (see Acts 2:17–21). As Psalm 45 spoke of the anointed king's "companions" (*metochous*) (Heb. 1:9; see 3:14), so the congregation had become the Holy Spirit's "companions" (*metochous*)[14] as he worked miracles among them. When apostates fail to "hold fast" the church's confession, they demonstrate that, despite the Spirit's gracious power at work *in the Christian community* through word and miracle, they (like the wilderness generation) "were not united with those who listened in faith" (4:2, my translation). Subsequent repentance and restoration are "impossible" (6:4) because such high-handed repudiation of Christ amounts to "crucifying once again the Son of God" in utter contempt (6:6), implicitly denying that he "offered himself without blemish to God" (9:14) to "bear the sins of many" (9:28).

The third warning passage (Heb. 10:26–31) picks up elements of the previous passages. Like 2:1–4, it contrasts the sanctions imposed by the

---

13 Noel Weeks, "Admonition and Error in Hebrews," *WTJ* 39, no. 1 (1976): 72–80; Martin Emmrich, "Hebrews 6:4–6—Again! (A Pneumatological Inquiry)," *WTJ* 65, no. 1 (2003): 83–95; George H. Guthrie, "Hebrews," in *Commentary on the New Testament Use of the Old Testament,* ed. G. K. Beale and D. A. Carson (Grand Rapids, MI: Baker, 2007), 962.

14 When used with *metochos* (partner, companion), a noun (or pronoun) in the genitive may refer to that which is shared (Heb. 3:1; 12:8) or to one or more individuals with whom something is shared (Heb. 1:9; see Ps. 118:63 LXX [119:63 ET]; Eccl. 4:10 LXX; Luke 5:7).

law of Moses to the "much worse punishment" (10:29) that will befall those who "go on sinning deliberately after receiving the knowledge of the truth" (10:26).[15] As in 6:4–6, the reason for the heightened severity of sanction for apostasy under the new covenant is the contempt that it heaps on Jesus, on his costly sacrifice, and on the Holy Spirit's witness: "one who has *trampled* underfoot the Son of God, and has *profaned* the blood of the covenant by which he was sanctified, and has *outraged* the Spirit of grace" (10:29). This warning reinforces the exhortation to hold fast "the confession of our hope" (10:23), to stimulate one another to love and good works, to continue meeting together, and to encourage each other (10:24–25). The terrifying, eternally deadly consequences of apostasy underscore the urgency of encouraging each other to persist in faith.

Our author, with pastoral wisdom and sensitivity, follows the dire warnings in Hebrews 6 and 10 with reassurances of his confidence that his hearers, having previously demonstrated courageous faith and compassion, will endure in their pilgrimage, avoiding the drift that ends in apostasy (6:9–12; 10:32–39). He writes to alert them to the risk but not to alarm them into insecurity about God's faithfulness. "Though we speak in this way, yet in your case, beloved, we feel sure of better things—things that belong to salvation. For God is not unjust so as to overlook your work and the love that you have shown for his name in serving the saints, as you still do" (6:9–10). They had suffered for their faith and identified with others enduring persecution (10:32–34), so their track record of trust under trial must now be extended through the present and into the future (10:35–39).

The Positive Examples of Enduring Faith

The encouragement in Hebrews 6:12 to imitate "those who through faith and patience inherit the promises" would be an ideal segue to the catalogue of Old Testament believers that finally appears in Hebrews 11. In Hebrews 6, however, Abraham alone is introduced as

---

15 "Sinning deliberately" (*hekousiōs hamartanontōn*) here refers to apostasy, knowledgeable and intentional repudiation of the gospel, which one once confessed to be true.

the representative of this company of the faith filled (6:13–18), and the focus is not on Abraham's faith (see 11:8–19) but on the oath by which God fortified the patriarch's trust. Why the apparent delay in cataloguing the "great cloud of witnesses" who populate the pages of the Old Testament? Perhaps because our minds must first be saturated with the glorious truth of the perfect priesthood and reconciling ministry of Jesus, the high priest of our confession (6:19–10:18). Once we have seen the perfection of Christ's priesthood, we are prepared to follow the footsteps of faith in Hebrews 11.

The catalogue of the ancient company of the faithful, when it arrives, is introduced by the citation of Habakkuk 2:3–4 (augmented from Isa. 26:20–21) in Hebrews 10:37–39. Habakkuk's prophetic word, despite its brevity, functions as the interpretive paradigm for the whole survey of faith-formed choices and actions throughout the era of promise. From the Habakkuk text, Hebrews draws four insights about the faith that pleases God.

First, faith focuses on the future, trusting that God is faithful to fulfill his promises of coming blessing:

> Yet a little while,
>   and the coming one *will come* and will not delay. (10:37)

This future focus is reinforced in the description of faith as "the reality [*hypostasis*] of *what is hoped for*, the proof [*elengkos*] of *what is not seen* [*ou blepomenōn*]" (11:1 CSB).[16] Noah's faith-motivated construction of the ark was prompted by God's warning about "things *not yet seen* [*tōn mēdepō blepomenōn*]" (NASB, NIV) or "events as yet unseen" (ESV), namely, the coming flood (11:7). The faith of Abraham, Sarah, and others led to their reliance on God's faithfulness to keep his promises in a distant future that they "greeted . . . from afar" (11:13).

16 See Dennis E. Johnson, *Hebrews*, in *Hebrews–Revelation*, vol. 12 of *ESVEC*, ed. Iain M. Duguid, James M. Hamilton Jr., and Jay Sklar (Crossway, IL: Wheaton, 2018), 162, for an argument that in Heb. 11:1 faith is described not in terms of subjective confidence but in terms of the objective reality that is faith's ground and warrant.

Second, the Habakkuk citation connects faith with *righteousness*. By accepting Abel's sacrifice, offered in faith, God testified that Abel was "righteous" (11:4). Noah's construction of the ark constituted him "an heir of the righteousness that comes by faith" (11:7). When the Old Testament characterizes individuals as "righteous," it is attributed to their faith. When Scripture speaks of their faith, it announces their right standing before God. Hebrews does not draw from Habakkuk 2:4 the sharp Pauline distinction between righteous standing received by *grace through faith*, on the one hand, and the pursuit of vindication through *one's own works*, on the other (Rom. 1:16–17; Gal. 3:11–14). Yet the Old Testament individuals whom our author selects for comment are by no means exemplary in character and conduct, as his hearers know well. Scripture does not conceal the sometimes faltering faith of Abraham and Sarah (Gen. 17:17–18; 18:12 with Heb. 11:11–12), Moses (Ex. 2:14–15 with Heb. 11:27), Gideon (Judg. 6:11–27, 36–40), or Barak (Judg. 4:6–10), nor does it gloss over the moral failures of Jephthah, Samson, or David. Despite their fluctuating faith and faithfulness, God commended them as righteous—through faith.

Third, faith stands in antithesis to "shrinking back" (*hypostellō* in 10:38; *hypostolē* in 10:39).[17] This is Habakkuk's terminology (LXX) for what Hebrews has warned against in various ways: drifting (2:1), neglecting God's word (2:3), hardening one's heart to God's voice (3:7–8, 13), falling away (3:12; 6:6), failing to obtain (4:1; 12:15), becoming sluggish (5:11; 6:12), throwing away one's confidence (10:35), growing weary and fainthearted (12:3, 5), and rejecting him who speaks (12:26–27). Instead of shrinking back, faith *endures* despite the difficulties entailed in trusting and the delay in God's fulfillment of his promises. Here the concept of "endurance" or "perseverance" takes its place alongside faith. The original audience has already "endured" (*hypomenō*) sufferings (10:32) and needs "endurance" (*hypomonē*) in the present and future (10:36).

17 Elsewhere, this word group describes avoiding action out of cowardice (Deut. 1:17 LXX; Acts 20:20, 27; Gal. 2:12).

They must run their race of faith with "endurance," strengthened by their view of Jesus, who "endured" both the cross and sinners' hostility (12:1–3).

Fourth, faith receives *God's good pleasure*. Since God has "no pleasure" (*ouk eudokei*)[18] in the one who shrinks back, the inverse is also true: God takes pleasure in the person of faith. When the Hebrew Scriptures say that Enoch and Noah "walked with God" (Gen. 5:22, 24; 6:9), the Septuagint interprets this as their "pleasing [*euaresteō*] God" (Gen. 5:22, 24; 6:9 LXX). God's pleasure displays their faith (Heb. 11:5), for "without faith it is impossible to please [God]" (11:6). The biblical record of these believers' lives constitutes God's testimony on their behalf. The repetition of the verb *martyreō* ("commend"), with God as the implied or stated subject, shows that the Old Testament narratives are God's verbal witness in defense of the ancients who believed and acted on his promises:[19]

- "For by [faith] the people of old received their commendation [*emartyrēthēsan*]" (11:2).
- "By faith Abel . . . was commended [*emartyrēthē*] as righteous, God commending [*martyrountos*] him by accepting his gifts" (11:4).
- "Before [Enoch] was taken he was commended [*memartyrētai*] as having pleased [*euarestēkenai*][20] God" (11:5).
- "And all these, though commended [*martyrēthentes*] through their faith, did not receive what was promised" (11:39).

18   The only other appearances of *eudokeō* in Hebrews are in the citation of and commentary on Ps. 40:6–8 LXX in Heb. 10:5–10, which (a) announces that God has "taken no pleasure" (*ouk eudokēsas*) in animal sacrifices (10:6, 8) and (b) introduces as their replacement Christ's offering of his body in fulfillment of God's will, recorded in "the scroll of the book" (10:7)—that is, prophesied in the Old Testament Scripture.

19   This point is made in other words by the comment that, because the patriarch longed for a heavenly country, "God *is not ashamed* to be called their God" (11:16).

20   As the ESV wording—"has . . . pleasure" (10:38) and "having pleased" (11:5)—indicates, the verbs *eudokeō* and *euaresteō* belong to the same semantic domain. *Eudokeō* expresses the response of the individual who "is pleased with something or someone," while *euaresteō* refers to the individual who causes or evokes another's good pleasure. "Εὐδοκέω" and "εὐαρεστέω" in L&N 25.87, 25:93; see also the entries in BAGD 318, 319.

Moreover, just as God gives testimony on behalf of those who have trusted him, so also, through the Old Testament text, they constitute a "cloud of witnesses" (12:1) who attest his faithfulness (11:4, 20–22).

Space constraints prevent our surveying, one by one, the ancient people of faith who are recalled in Hebrews 11. With respect to the author's theology of faith, however, one further motif must be discussed: faith demands endurance because *faith is costly*, eliciting opposition and bringing suffering, alienation, and loss. Abraham responded in faith when God called him to leave the security of country and kindred (Gen. 12:1) and travel to an unknown destination (Heb. 11:8). That act of faith meant sojourning *for his entire life* as a stranger and exile (11:9, 13). Others, by faith, endured homelessness and destitution: "They went about in skins of sheep and goats, destitute, afflicted, mistreated—of whom the world was not worthy—wandering about in deserts and mountains, and in dens and caves of the earth" (11:37–38). Some of the Hebrew Christians also lost property for Jesus's sake (10:34).

The cost of faith may include social alienation, abusive treatment, violence, and even death. Abel, whose murder begins the roster of ancient believers (11:4), is only the first of many who "were tortured, refusing to accept release, so that they might rise again to a better life. Others suffered mocking and flogging, and even chains and imprisonment. They were stoned, they were sawn in two, they were killed with the sword" (11:35–37). For the original audience, the price of trusting Jesus had not yet escalated to martyrdom (12:4), but some had suffered public humiliation and imprisonment (10:32–34; 13:3). The danger of being exposed as a Christian may tempt some to neglect Christian gatherings (10:25) and refuse hospitality to strangers (13:2). They needed to heed Moses's example of faith, by which he "refused to be called the son of Pharaoh's daughter, choosing rather to be mistreated with the people of God than to enjoy the fleeting pleasures of sin. He considered *the reproach of Christ* greater wealth than the treasures of Egypt, for he was looking to the reward" (11:24–26). Our author connects Moses's choice to his original audience by labeling the Israelites' hardships "the reproach [*oneidismon*] of Christ." Later he challenges his hearers: Since "Jesus suffered outside the gate" (repudiated by his people and their leaders), we must "go to him outside the camp and bear the reproach [*oneidismon*] he endured" (13:12–13). The reproach endured by Jesus the Messiah marks the finale of the author's survey of the ancient people of faith. While they surround us as a cloud of witnesses to attest God's faithfulness (12:1), *Jesus himself* is the one on whom our eyes must be fixed:

> looking to Jesus, the founder [or "champion," *archēgos*][21] and perfecter of our faith, who for the joy that was set before him endured the cross, despising the shame, and is seated at the right hand of the throne of God. Consider him who endured from sinners such hostility against himself, so that you may not grow weary or fainthearted. (12:2–3)

The author's rich exposition of the Son's incarnation and reconciling mission has shown Jesus to be the *object* of our faith, the "high priest of our confession" (3:1) through whose mediation we may draw near to God (4:14–16). Because he suffered when tempted, Jesus is the *helper* to those whose faith is undergoing trial (2:17–18; 4:15). Now we learn that Jesus is also the supreme *example* of enduring faith, who looked beyond the shame, pain, and death that he would suffer on the cross to glimpse "the joy that was set before him," the reward of his sacrificial obedience. Hebrews identified that reward in its citation of Psalm 22, which opens with a cry of dereliction ("My God, my God, why have you forsaken me?") but abruptly turns from lament to celebration with

> I will tell of your name to my brothers;
>   in the midst of *the* congregation I will praise you." (Ps. 22:22,
>   cited in Heb. 2:12)

---

21 See p. 126 for my discussion of *archēgos* in 2:10 in chap. 6.

The prospect of "bringing many sons to glory" fortified the Son for his suffering (2:10). Foreseeing this joyful outcome and trusting the Father's promise, our champion endured the pain and shame of the cross and the rejection and abuse of sinners. Now he helps his suffering pilgrim people as they make their way through this world's wilderness.

Corporate Solidarity

This "word of exhortation" (13:22) is replete with *exhortations* to persevering faith in Jesus. Endurance depends on corporate accountability and mutual support. Believers do not thrive, and may not even survive, if they attempt their pilgrimage in solitude. They must exhort each other daily, lest any fall away from the living God, deceived and hardened by sin (3:12–14). They must not neglect their gathering in a messianic "synagogue" (*episynagogē*, 10:25), since this is the venue in which they encourage each other and stir up each other to love and good deeds (10:24). The hearers' earlier courage in identifying with fellow believers who suffered public humiliation must be maintained into the present (10:32–34; 13:1–3).

Just as encouragement and hope can be contagious, so also can discouragement and doubt. Therefore, our author urges, "See to it that no one fails to obtain the grace of God; that no 'root of bitterness' springs up and causes trouble, and by it many become defiled" (12:15). He draws the expression "root of bitterness" from Moses's warning to the Israelite generation soon to enter the land (Deut. 29:18 [29:17 LXX]). It refers to those who would secretly worship false gods, confident that their rebellion will escape God's notice and retribution. One individual's doubt and defiance can infect and defile many. The health of the whole community is at risk when any of its members begin to drift. So the whole congregation must proactively protect one another from "an evil, unbelieving heart" (Heb. 3:12). Those who are weak and wavering must be strengthened like injured limbs that hinder athletes' competition: "Therefore lift your drooping hands and strengthen your weak knees, and make straight paths for your feet, so that what is lame may not be put out of joint but rather be healed" (12:12–13). Leaders have responsibilities, of course. In the past, the congregation had leaders who faithfully spoke God's word and set an example of enduring faith (13:7). In the present, they must also submit to their current leaders, recognizing that they keep watch over their souls and are accountable to God (13:17). Yet the exhortations to mutual accountability and mutual encouragement that punctuate this sermon are addressed not only to elders or pastors but to all who affirm and hold fast to their common confession of hope. Endurance in faith is a communal calling.

Conclusion

As we pilgrims traverse this world's wilderness, our endurance in faith is not effortless. Sharing the reproach of Christ is not painless. Christ's followers must "*strive* to enter [God's] rest, so that no one may fall by the same sort of disobedience" (4:11). To hold fast their confession, believers must "with confidence draw near to the throne of grace, that we may receive mercy and find grace to help in time of need" (4:16).

Their stamina to endure can only come from Jesus, the high priest who has shared their experience of weakness and testing and who ever lives and ever prays for them. So the secret of survival in the wilderness is to "consider Jesus, the apostle and high priest of our confession" (3:1), to look "to Jesus, the founder and perfecter of our faith" (12:2), and to "consider him who endured from sinners such hostility against himself" (12:3) for the sake of rescuing us from death and the devil and reconciling us to God.

Conclusion

HYMN WRITER Isaac Watts asked,

> Is this vile world a friend to grace,
> to help me on to God?[1]

The answer, of course, is "Certainly not!" The world—rebellious humankind—hated Jesus and hates his followers (John 15:18–19). By faith in God's word, Noah built the ark, saved his family, and "condemned the world" (Heb. 11:7). The "world" that expelled people of faith, to wander in deserts and mountains and seek shelter in caves, "was not worthy" of those homeless heirs of God's eternal kingdom (11:38). God's pilgrim people are not in friendly territory.

Yet Israel's experience with Moses and the sermon to the Hebrews agree that the only route from the house of bondage to the heavenly city runs through the hostile wilderness, which bristles with threats and tests of faith. The danger of drifting away, of falling short, of failing to hold fast, looms large. For the Hebrew Christians who first heard this sermon, the lure was to return to the old covenant institutions—priesthood, sanctuary, sacrifice—of their youth, which had ancient precedent and even (at one time) God's authorization. By returning, they could hope to avoid ostracism and reproach—and perhaps even chains and death.

We in the twenty-first century may be tempted to drift away in other directions. In the West, young adults raised in Christian homes

---

1 Isaac Watts, "Am I a Soldier of the Cross?," 1724.

and churches may react to the failures of parents and pastors by "deconstructing" the faith they were taught and rebuilding one more in tune with the times, less at odds with their surroundings. Postmodern expressive individualism persuasively urges us to listen to our inner voices instead of to the voice of the Lord speaking from above. Naturalistic determinism offers a universe comfortably devoid of personal accountability but also lacking transcendent purpose. Distractions and devices, our culture's version of Egypt's treasures, offer delights and diversions more appealing than the reproach of Christ. And elsewhere around the globe, the world displays its unfriendliness to grace in more overtly aggressive ways.

Hebrews is God's gift to weary pilgrims, to feed our faith and sustain our stamina as we wend our way through this world's hostile wilderness toward the celestial city. Hebrews is meat to be chewed by the mature, not milk merely imbibed by babies. But the effort it demands is amply repaid by the Spirit of grace in the nourishment we receive as we look to Jesus, the apostle and high priest of our confession and the champion and perfecter of our faith. Because Jesus is better—better than prophets, angels, Moses, Joshua, Aaron, the old covenant, the tabernacle, bulls and goats, and Canaan—we can and must hold fast our confession of hope in him. Because Jesus's death has perfected our consciences and opened wide the way into God's heavenly sanctuary, we can draw near the throne of grace to receive the grace and help we need to endure in faith, offering grateful and acceptable worship. Because Jesus is the priest perfected forever, always living and always praying for us, our salvation to the uttermost is secure.

So Hebrews calls us to press on to maturity together, under the blessing of the God of peace through our risen Savior and shepherd:

> Now may the God of peace who brought again from the dead our Lord Jesus, the great shepherd of the sheep, by the blood of the eternal covenant, equip you with everything good that you may do his will, working in us that which is pleasing in his sight, through Jesus Christ, to whom be glory forever and ever. Amen. (13:20–21)

Recommended Resources

Commentaries

Attridge, Harold W. *The Epistle to the Hebrews*. Hermeneia. Philadelphia: Fortress, 1989.

Brown, Raymond. *The Message of Hebrews: Christ Above All*. The Bible Speaks Today. Downers Grove, IL: InterVarsity Press, 1982.

Bruce, F. F. *The Epistle to the Hebrews*. NICNT. Rev. ed. Grand Rapids, MI: Eerdmans, 1990.

Guthrie, George H. "Hebrews." Pages 919–95 in *Commentary on the New Testament Use of the Old Testament*. Edited by G. K. Beale and D. A. Carson. Grand Rapids, MI: Baker Academic, 2007.

Hagner, Donald A. *Encountering the Book of Hebrews: An Exposition*. Encountering Biblical Studies. Grand Rapids, MI: Baker Academic, 2002.

Harris, Dana M. *Hebrews*. Exegetical Guide to the Greek New Testament. Nashville: B&H Academic, 2019.

Hughes, Philip Edgcumbe. *A Commentary on the Epistle to the Hebrews*. Grand Rapids, MI: Eerdmans, 1977.

Johnson, Dennis E. *Hebrews*. In *Hebrews–Revelation*, 19–217. Vol. 12 of *ESVEC*. Edited by Iain M. Duguid, James M. Hamilton Jr., and Jay Sklar. Wheaton, IL: Crossway, 2018.

Johnson, Luke Timothy. *Hebrews: A Commentary*. NTL. Louisville: Westminster John Knox, 2006.

Lane, William L. *Hebrews 1–8*. WBC 47A. Dallas: Word, 1991.

Lane, William L. *Hebrews 9–13*. WBC 47B. Dallas: Word, 1991.

Montefiore, Hugh. *The Epistle to the Hebrews*. HNTC. San Francisco: Harper & Row, 1964.

Phillips, Richard D. *Hebrews*. Reformed Expository Commentary. Phillipsburg, NJ: P&R, 2006.

Schreiner, Thomas R. *Commentary on Hebrews*. BTCP. Nashville: Holman Reference, 2015.

Westcott, Brooke Foss. *The Epistle to the Hebrews: The Greek Text with Notes and Essays*. London: Macmillan, 1920. Reprinted by Grand Rapids, MI: Eerdmans, 1970.

Monographs

Hughes, Graham. *Hebrews and Hermeneutics: The Epistle to the Hebrews as a New Testament Example of Biblical Interpretation*. Cambridge: Cambridge University Press, 1979.

Kim, Lloyd. *Polemic in the Book of Hebrews: Anti-Judaism, Anti-Semitism, Supercession?* Princeton Theological Monograph Series. Eugene, OR: Pickwick, 2006.

Lane, William L. *Call to Commitment: Responding to the Message of Hebrews*. Nashville: Thomas Nelson, 1985.

Lee, Gregory W. *Today When You Hear His Voice: Scripture, the Covenants, and the People of God*. Grand Rapids, MI: Eerdmans, 2016.

Lindars, Barnabas. *The Theology of the Letter to the Hebrews*. New Testament Theology. Cambridge: Cambridge University Press, 1991.

Vos, Geerhardus. *The Teaching of the Epistle to the Hebrews*. Grand Rapids, MI: Eerdmans, 1956.

Articles

DeYoung, Kevin. "Divine Impassibility and the Passion of Christ in the Book of Hebrews." *WTJ* 68, no. 1 (2006): 41–50.

Emmrich, Martin. "Hebrews 6:4–6—Again! (A Pneumatological Inquiry)." *WTJ* 65, no. 1 (2003): 83–95.

France, R. T. "The Writer of Hebrews as a Biblical Expositor." *TynBul* 47, no. 2 (1996): 245–76.

Gaffin, Richard B., Jr., "The Priesthood of Christ: A Servant in the Sanctuary." Pages 49–68 in *The Perfect Saviour: Key Themes in Hebrews*. Edited by Jonathan Griffiths. Nottingham: Inter-Varsity Press, 2012. Pages 291–305 in Richard B. Gaffin, Jr., *Word & Spirit: Selected Writings in Biblical and Systematic Theology*. Edited by David Garner and Guy Waters. Philadelphia: Westminster Seminary Press, 2023.

Hughes, John J. "Hebrews IX 15ff. and Galatians III.15ff.: A Study in Covenant Practice and Procedure." *NovT* 21, no. 1 (1979): 27–96.

Stanley, Steve. "The Structure of Hebrews from Three Perspectives." *TynBul* 45, no. 2 (1994): 245–71.

Vos, Geerhardus. "Hebrews, the Epistle of the Diatheke." Pages 161–233 in Geerhardus Vos, *Redemptive History and Biblical Interpretation: The Shorter Writings of Geerhardus Vos*. Edited by Richard B. Gaffin Jr. Phillipsburg, NJ: P&R, 1980.

Vos, Geerhardus. "The Priesthood of Christ in the Epistle to the Hebrews." Pages 126–60 in Geerhardus Vos, *Redemptive History and Biblical Interpretation: The Shorter Writings of Geerhardus Vos*. Edited by Richard B. Gaffin Jr. Phillipsburg, NJ: P&R, 1980.

Weeks, Noel. "Admonition and Error in Hebrews." *WTJ* 39, no. 1 (1976): 72–80.

General Index

Scripture Index

New Testament Theology

Edited by Thomas R. Schreiner and Brian S. Rosner, this series presents clear, scholarly overviews of the main theological themes of each book of the New Testament, examining what they reveal about God and his relation to the world in the context of the overarching biblical narrative.

For more information, visit **crossway.org**.